WHEELSPIN

THE AUTHOR IN ACTION

Photo : Louis Klemanjaski

THE FOUR M.G. CARS WITH WHICH THE AUTHOR HAD MOST OF HIS TRIALS' EXPERIENCES

1. THE J2 MIDGET
Photo : Logan, Birmingham

2. THE P TYPE MIDGET
Photo : Brunell

3. THE N MAGNETTE
Photo : Brunell

4. THE " BLOWN " PB MIDGET
Photo : Louis Klemantaski

WHEELSPIN

*Competition Motoring
from the Driver's Seat*

BY

C. A. N. MAY

G T FOULIS & CO LTD
HENLEY-ON-THAMES
OXFORDSHIRE

First Published 1945
Second Edition 1945
Reprinted . . 1946
Reprinted . . 1948
Classic reprint 1971

© C. A. N. May 1945, 71

ISBN 0 85429 134 2

Printed in Great Britain by
Biddles Limited, Guildford, Surrey

AUTHOR'S PREFACE TO THE CLASSIC REPRINT

IN the years immediately before the Second World War, which is the period of motor sport dealt with in this book, club racing—today practised almost every weekend of the season on tracks all over the country—was non-existent. Racing of any sort was confined to the old Brooklands track, the narrow parkland circuit at Donington, together with occasional forays at Crystal Palace.

Because of this, the main pastime of the clubmen of those days was "Trials". Major trials events used to attract entries nearly as large as are today received for race meetings at Silverstone, Goodwood, or Brands. Entries usually consisted of only mildly modified (and, up to 1938, "knobbly-tyre" equipped) versions of the small two-seater sports cars of the day. Most popular of these were the various MG models, the Le Mans-type Singers, "chain gang" Frazer Nashes, sporting derivatives of the ubiquitous Austin Seven (including the famous "Grasshoppers"), Rileys, Triumphs and a sprinkling of early V8 Fords, with the V8 Allards arriving spectacularly on the scene shortly before motor sport folded up with the onset of War.

Specialization leading to the purpose-built, mainly small-engined, "all-of-a-kind" machines contesting today's National Formula events, came in the early 1950s. This development, together with a swing of interest among younger clubmen to circuit racing, finally brought an end to some of the really great features of trials events. The regular (often factory sponsored) teams disappeared. And, perhaps more important, the terrific, but always friendly, rivalry born of inter-team competition disappeared with them.

But even today evidence comes regularly to hand that the tremendous reputations of the "Musketeer" MGs, the "Grasshopper" Austins and many others, lives on. And no less well-remembered are the great drivers of the time: R. A. Macdermid, the late Maurice Toulmin, Syd Allard, colourful Jack Baston and a host of others. It gives me great pleasure that my story of the men and machines of a never to be repeated chapter of motoring history, will now reach a new age of enthusiasts.

C. A. N. May

Solihull, Warwickshire.

1971.

CONTENTS

LIST OF ILLUSTRATIONS

CHAPTER I

"Non-Stop" Begins

"ONCE upon a time there stood a policeman at the finish of a London–Exeter motor trial, good naturedly, but with some amazement, watching strings of competitors checking-in, covered with mud, after an all-night and all-day run, finishing once again in darkness. He said to a bystander, ' How many more of these lunatics are there to arrive, and why do they do it ? ' " (Extract from *The Autocar*, January 4th, 1935.)

Why do they do it ? How often one heard this question from interested spectators who had seen cars and their crews participating in that particular form of sport with motor-cars that we, the participants, called simply " Trials." In point of fact, a full and satisfying answer can be given in straightforward and entirely non-technical language. To produce that answer right away, however, would rather savour of putting the cart before the horse, because a lot of folk, keen enough motorists though they be, will have had no physical contact with this form of motor sport at all, and, before they go on to ask why we did it, they will first want some elucidation as to just what " it " comprised.

The majority of people find it rather hard to visualize a form of competition between motor-cars in which the ability to go " faster than the other man " and to be " first past the post " is NOT a primary requirement for success.

In this particular form of motor sport we used to call simply " Trials," there was no question of getting there first. Let us try this line of approach to the matter. That word " trials " should have before it a qualifying adjective. In the earlier days of the sport, that qualifying adjective was " reliability "—a test of the reliability of a particular motor vehicle while being driven over a prescribed route and to a set time schedule. Notice that " to a set time schedule "—NOT " in the shortest possible time."

But that was in the early days. As the mechanical development of the motor-car progressed over the years, to an ever-increasing pitch of efficiency, the degree of reliability experienced reached a point where, under all NORMAL touring conditions, it came to be taken for granted.

The next step, then, was for organizers of trials to present prospective competitors with AB-normal conditions, and the cars were diverted more and more from the main and secondary roads on to by-ways, cart-tracks, and disused "Roman roads," and over moorland tracks and bridle-paths. In the process the nature of the events changed, so that motor trials became tests of the capability, rather than the reliability, of the motor vehicle. The more suitable qualifying adjective to the word "trials" at this stage was "sporting," the whole thing developing into cross-country runs, of ever-increasing severity.

In the matter of capability, it is not all that long time ago that an unaided NON-STOP climb of hills such as Porlock, in North Somerset, to name perhaps the best-known example, was considered to be outside the capabilities of many of the cars then in production. I remember well an occasion, within the last twenty-five years, when my own father, although a motorist of long experience, fought shy of climbing Porlock, preferring the more easily graded and specially constructed toll-road. Yet he had a big American car, considered to be powerful in its day. It was Porlock's reputation that beat him.

As the trial developed from "reliability" to "sporting," trials routes were planned to include hills of the Porlock type, and it became a requirement of competitors that hey should climb these hills non-stop and without outside assistance. As the motor vehicle increased steadily in efficiency, the Porlock type of hill steadily lost its "terrors," and a new difficulty was created for competitors by cars being brought to a standstill at the foot of a "non-stop" hill, the unaided non-stop climb then having to be made from a standing-start, quite a different kettle of fish in the case of a really steep hill.

The practice of cars having to take the non-stop hills from a standing-start became almost universal, but, even so, the days when the Porlock type constituted any sort of an obstacle to the man who drove regularly in competition had passed long before I had my first practical contact with trials, which was early in 1933.

At this stage the nature of the surfaces of the non-stop hills, rather than the severity of their gradients, had become the determining factor as to whether cars could be persuaded to "maintain forward motion relative to the course" in these sections. At the stage when I entered trials, sheer gradient

alone, without the combination of a bad surface, rarely stopped
the average trials car, unless it were badly driven, or mechanically " off colour." Inability to obtain a grip for the driving
wheels (wheelspin) caused a car to come to a standstill, rather
than any lack of power to overcome sheer steepness.

Now lots of people, keen enough motorists though they be,
rarely venture off the main roads. Even so, many of them will
have had experience of how quickly, under adverse conditions,
the motor vehicle, even in its most modern form, can be brought
to a halt and rendered ineffective to proceed under its own power
and without outside assistance, if they have had occasion to take
out their cars after a heavy fall of snow.

Change the snow into mud and you begin to get an idea of
the nature of the obstacles which competitors in the latter-day
trials set out to surmount. Can I blame you, then, if you join
that puzzled policeman referred to in my first paragraph, and
ask, " Why do they do it? "—or, more correctly, " Why DID
they do it? " because all forms of motor sport ceased on the
outbreak of war.

Here is your answer, given by a man who, during the eight
to ten years before the present war, was a leading figure in the
sport of motor trials and one of our cleverest and most
experienced drivers—J. Maurice Toulmin.

In an article published in *The Autocar* of November 19th, 1937,
under the title " Why Not Enter for a Trial? ", Toulmin wrote :

" Ever since normal motoring ceased to be an adventure
(except very occasionally), reliability trials, hill climbs, and
rallies have become a popular sport, in which the enthusiast
can enjoy the thrills of strange adventure and satisfy that competitive instinct which is present in all of us.

" That camaraderie of the road, once to be found whenever
two or three car owners were gathered together, and always on
top when anyone was in trouble on the road, is still perpetuated
in the sporting side of motoring. That is one of its biggest
appeals."

Since I have been at some pains to emphasize that there was
no question of " getting there first," some perplexity may still
exist as to just where the competitive angle did come in, and by
what method the winners were determined. Theoretically the
winner—in trials parlance the man recording " The Best Performance of the Day "—was the competitor who made non-stop

ascents of every one of the hills and sections of track scheduled to be so climbed. In practice it was rare, though not entirely unknown, for only one driver to succeed in climbing every one of the non-stop hills, so that there was always included at least one " against-the-watch " manœuvre. There were wide variations of the " driving," or " special," or " tie-deciding " test, but usually a good deal of involved manœuvring in restricted spaces, with frequent changes of direction from forward to reverse, and forward again, was called for.

So where more than one competitor was successful on all of the non-stop hills there WAS the requirement to " go faster than the other man," but ONLY in the executing of that particular manœuvre, and the PRIMARY requirement for success was the ability to make non-stop climbs, from a standing-start, of course, of all the sections so scheduled, since it availed a man nothing to be, perhaps, seconds faster than the next best in the special test if he had failed on a hill.

My own interest in cars, and in motor sport in particular, dated back to schooldays, but it was not until late in 1932, at the age of twenty-two, that I first seriously considered exchanging the rôle of enthusiastic spectator for that of actual competitor. To this end I purchased one of the 8 h.p., 847 c.c. J2 model M.G. Midgets.

The little M.G. was a leading example of the type of small-engined, high-performance car, of sports type, usually carrying slightly sketchy, open two-seater bodywork, much in favour for participation in the trials of the day. The J2, first out on the market in August 1932, set a new standard in small sports car design and performance, and represented a direct outcome of the M.G. Car Co.'s regular participation in racing events, both at home and abroad.

In general external appearance the new M.G. bore a strong resemblance to the company's successful racing machines, even to the point of being equipped with the rather skimpy, non-valanced, " cycle-type " mudguards favoured for racing purposes. For competition purposes these little guards had the double advantage of saving weight and aiding manœuvreability, but under more normal touring conditions were found to give insufficient protection to the driver and passenger in adverse weather, and later long, sweeping, fully valanced mudguards of more conventional pattern were fitted.

The engine, too, bore the stamp of experience gained in the racing field, the cylinder-head being quite new, with the inlet and exhaust ports on opposite sides of the head, a layout much favoured in engines designed to give high performance. On the inlet side two carburettors were used.

It is ancient history now that the initial batch of this highly successful, and affectionately remembered, little sports car suffered more than the average number of " teething " troubles, while there was, in addition, a conspicuous and most disheartening lack of the anticipated high range of performance. While being road-tested by the leading weekly motoring journals the new M.G. had been found capable of a maximum speed in the neighbourhood of 80 m.p.h., but the sample that came into my hands had a hard struggle to reach 65 m.p.h. No point will be served by going into the whys and wherefores in this narrative, sufficient is it to say that the problems encountered in the first batch of the J2's to come into the hands of the public were quickly and satisfactorily overcome, and the model then, as I have said already, set a new standard for small sports cars.

I persevered with my car for a month or two, loath to believe that I had been " sold a pup," but after making a trip into the Cotswolds, along with some already experienced drivers, to see at first hand, for the first time, the type of non-stop hill at that time being used in trials, and having the M.G. stop on every hill for sheer lack of power, patience could be contained no longer. The car was rushed back to Abingdon, where was sited the M.G. factory, acrimonious correspondence was entered into, and my entry into the sport of motor trials postponed indefinitely.

My first practical contact with the sport, in consequence, was obtained in the rôle of passenger, instead of driver, when I rode in H. K. Crawford's 1271 c.c. Wolseley Hornet Special, in the 1933 London–Land's End Trial.

The " Land's End " ranked as one of the classics of the trials world, and was always held at Easter, with the start scheduled for the evening of Good Friday. The " Land's End " was a direct link with the early " reliability " days of the sport and was one of the few long-distance events still staged, the favourite type of trial in the early 1930's being the so-called " half-day " trial, providing anything up to eight or ten non-stop hills, and one or two special tests, in a mileage of under one hundred, often nearer fifty.

Crawford, a Wolverhampton man, and myself had struck up an acquaintance, on the basis of a mutual interest in motor sport, during regular attendance at the Birmingham Ice-Skating Rink. I had not, however, had occasion to pursue this friendship outside of these meetings, so that I was mildly, though agreeably, surprised when Crawford telephoned me at business one morning, shortly before Easter (1933), to tell me that he had entered the Hornet Special for the forthcoming London–Land's End trial, and hoped to be able to persuade me to go along as passenger. (Trials regulations always called for a minimum of at least one adult passenger to be carried in the car throughout.) I needed no persuasion and agreed immediately to " make it a date."

When Crawford called at my house about tea-time on the Good Friday I knew in an instant, by his expression, that the car must have been giving trouble. I was right. Now it must, of course, be sheer coincidence—there can be no feasible explanation for the phenomena—but bitter experience has given rise to the belief that no matter how well a particular car may have been behaving, you have only to enter it for a trial, and equip it with competition numbers, for that car immediately to develop every imaginable mechanical disorder !

It does not make sense, I know, but the fact remains that Crawford's car had suddenly, almost at the eleventh hour, developed troubles not previously experienced. The whole wiring system had suddenly gone adrift, so that such peculiar things happened as the headlights coming on when the horn was operated. No sooner had that been sorted into shape than the cylinder-head gasket was discovered to be leaking badly, and the head was only got back into position with an hour or so to spare, the work having to be finished hurriedly, so that there was a number of oil leaks, while the head itself still needed further tightening down as it " settled," and, all in all, Crawford was a little chary of our prospects.

The start for the 1933 " Land's End " was from Heston airport. No untoward incidents befell us on the run down to there from my home at King's Norton, Birmingham, so that by the time Crawford and I arrived at the airport our hopes had risen a little. At the start I quickly began to catch something of the atmosphere of these big trials, and to sense the spell of adventure. More than three hundred cars were setting out through the night, being dispatched on their way at intervals

1934 "BRIGHTON-BEER"—R. A. MACDERMID (P-TYPE M.G. MIDGET)
AT THE SUMMIT OF HATHERLAND

Photo : " The Autocar "

1934 "ONE DAY SPORTING"—A. B. LANGLEY (LE MANS SINGER
NINE) WELL AWAY ON BAMFORD CLOUGH, UNDER THE EAGLE
EYE OF JACK WOODHOUSE (STANDING RIGHT)

of one minute, and as Crawford had sent in his entry for the event rather late, we were towards the tail-end of the long procession, not getting under way until about 3 a.m. on Easter Saturday morning.

The first part of the route was over main roads, the non-stop hills being attempted after the breakfast stop at Taunton, and in daylight. Just as Crawford and I were really settling down, the Hornet Special's engine suddenly faltered. Crawford drew the car in to the roadside, out we got, up went the bonnet, and following competitors swept by and left us. While I held a torch Crawford again tightened down the cylinder-head holding bolts and those of adjoining components, and withdrew the plugs, checked the points, and replaced them after cleaning. Fearfully we set off again.

Andover ; Amesbury ; time-check at Deptford (a margin of not more than ten minutes behind schedule permitted, and penalty for early arrival) ; a " break " for a cup of coffee, and a warm, at Willoughby Hedge ; Langport—were all passed without further incident. A mile or so outside Taunton, where an hour was scheduled for breakfast to be taken, the Hornet Special was brought to a halt, Crawford and I jacked up the rear axle, removed the two road-wheels, and replaced them with the two wheels shod with " competition " (knobbly) tyres which had been reposing on a bracket at the rear of the body.

The early promise of a fine sunny day was being amply fulfilled when we re-started after breakfast. Almost at once main roads were left behind, by a turning to the left, a little way beyond Bishop's Lydeard, on the road to Minehead and North Devon.

Through Elworthy, and by way of Raleigh's Cross, and down into Timberscombe, the engine-note of the Hornet Special never faltered, and as I read out the route-card directions—" fork left in front of garage, right at T-roads, and shortly fork left uphill " —Crawford and I excitedly braced ourselves for our first non-stop hill, Grabhurst. As had now become the custom, the car was brought to a standstill by an official of the organizing club, and when the preceding competitor's car had been cleared from the hill, Crawford was given the signal to pass the " Non-Stop Begins " notice, and make his attempt.

Admittedly Grabhurst was never much more than a " curtain-raiser," and was omitted from the route in later years as being too easy, but the psychological effect of a successful climb of the first of the non-stop hills is worth a lot, and for Crawford and me that morning, was terrific, so that confidence was fully restored.

But the fates had not finished with us, and that confidence was to be rudely shattered only a few miles farther on. Half-way up Porlock, no longer, of course, a non-stop hill, the Hornet suddenly faltered, slowed, struggled agonizingly, all but stopped, and then crawled spluttering to the summit. It was an awful moment : neither of us spoke. To have come so far. . . . Once again Crawford grappled with " the works," the backs of his hands now raw and bleeding from sharp contact with various of the engine's components.

At last, fearfully, he pressed the starter-button. The engine sprang into life at once and turned over evenly. Fate had dealt us her last blow. From that point onwards the Hornet went great guns, and Crawford drove it successfully on all of the non-stop hills, so that as we wound through Portreath and Porthtowan in gathering dusk, passed Hell's Mouth, and came down into Penzance, we agreed that it had been a grand adventure, moreover an adventure brought to a successful conclusion, which, at one time *en route*, had seemed impossible of achievement.

It was two tired but very happy people, rejoicing in memories which would never be entirely erased, that checked in at the Land's End Hotel that Easter Saturday evening, finishing, as they had started, in darkness.

The London–Edinburgh run at Whitsun proved nothing like such fun, and not just because the Hornet failed on one of the non-stop hills—the first at that—nor even because my breakfast, taken at Harrogate, violently disagreed with me. I just never " fell " for the " Edinburgh." Just the same, for the tyro that I was in 1933, it was first-class experience, even from the passenger's seat, and I was still a passenger.

To go back a bit chronologically, my J2 M.G. Midget, now capable in full measure of giving the anticipated high range of performance, had been returned to me by the factory even before the " Land's End." But I had not driven it in either the Land's End Trial or the " Edinburgh " for this reason.

Once in a while there comes, even from the best factories, and for no discernible reason, an " outlaw " car, and my first M.G. showed me, in a dozen different ways, it was such a car. Thus every time I said to myself that now I really would change from spectator (or passenger) to actual competitor, something would go wrong, until in early summer the car crashed, fortunately without personal injury.

That the car AS A TYPE had the right make-up for success in competition was obvious, not only from its performance in the hands of other drivers, but also from the fact that in between its bouts of " temperament " I had driven my own car (after it was put right, of course) on a number of local non-stop hills and romped up all of them. After the crash, therefore, I had no hesitation in arranging to buy another J2 type M.G. Midget.

During the spring and summer of 1933 I built up, in various ways, a fund of knowledge and experience which was going to stand me in good stead when eventually I should get started. As an observer on a non-stop hill in a trial organized by the Sutton Coldfield and North Birmingham Automobile Club, my " local " club (usually known as " Sunbac "), I saw something of the rocky-surfaced Derbyshire trials hills. Observing again, on a motor-cycle trial, I had my first introduction to the Stroud-Nailsworth-Minchinhampton area, a very favourite locale with the organizers of the shorter " half-day " trials.

In conversation with some of the experienced drivers, many of whom came from the Midlands and whom I got to know through Sunbac and through going on trials with Crawford, I picked up many helpful hints and tips on the preparing of my car for regular participation in trials. I learned, for example, that, in the case of the J2, it was a good thing to have the crown-wheel and bevel-pinion changed for a pair that gave a slightly lower set of gear-ratios, and this modification I had carried out to my car, before I entered it for the M.G. Car Club's Abingdon–Abingdon Trial on Saturday, September 9th, 1933.

From the M.G. factory, on the outskirts of Abingdon, there was a main-road run to Winchcombe, in the Cotswolds, where was sited the first time check. Among the experienced competition drivers whom I had been getting to know was a number who were doing their stuff, and doing it very well, on the J2 model M.G. Midgets. On the strength of a scarcely more than casual acquaintance with two of them who were already prominent in motor trials, J. A. Bastock and A. B. (Arch) Langley, I introduced myself, hesitantly, to leading M.G. exponent R. A. Macdermid. Macdermid was a consistently successful driver of long experience, having " served his apprenticeship " to the sport on motor-cycles (generally regarded as the finest "proving-ground" for success in motor sport). Together with Bastock, Langley, and Maurice Toulmin (mentioned at the beginning), Macdermid was putting the little M.G.s right in the forefront of the trials picture. Immediate rivals to the M.G.s were the newly introduced Sports Singer Nines, and I made the acquaintance of one of the leading figures in the Singer "camp," Harold M. Avery, well-known Cheltenham motor agent.

To continue the Abingdon Trial. At the foot of Cleeve Hill, almost on the outskirts of Cheltenham, a turning to the left led to Mill Lane, a favourite obstacle of the early thirties, upon the upper reaches of which was staged the first "against-the-watch" test—a "stop-and-go" test.

For the enthusiast who has not actually been in a trial, but has borne with me thus far, a further word of explanation may be welcome. The biggest bugbear of the average learner-driver, and of quite a few more experienced motorists also, is the business of getting the car into motion again after it has been brought to a standstill on a steep hill (facing up the gradient, of course). One always seems to want another pair of hands and feet, it appearing to be necessary to operate all the pedals, levers, and knobs on the car simultaneously, so that, nine times out of ten, at the moment of anticipated take-off, either the car runs gaily away downhill backwards or else leaps light-heartedly into the air like a startled rabbit, what time the engine stalls and then proves obstinate to start up again.

Visualize making your getaway on a surface of, say, slippery rock or mud, or, perhaps, loose gravel, not in your own time, but immediately upon the receipt of a given signal, and with the added requirement of not exceeding a "bogey" time in covering the first so many yards above the re-start point, and you have some idea of a "stop-and-go" or "re-start" test. Occasionally, as in the present instance, the engine would also be stopped when the car was brought to a halt at the appointed re-start line, being re-started at the fall of the flag (assuming that to be the pre-arranged signal), and the getaway then undertaken. This method was the exception, however, the car usually being held on the starting-line with the engine running, and being set into motion immediately upon the driver receiving the "go" signal.

On Mill Lane, in this 1933 "Abingdon," I gave a real beginner's exhibition. At the flag-fall the engine refused to start, and I panicked. Suddenly, as I pressed wildly on the starter-button, it burst into life. Off went the handbrake, in came the clutch, throttle wide open—and the car started to run away backwards down the hill. I had omitted the rather necessary precaution of engaging a gear ! Feverishly I tried to crash in a gear, my feet got tied up with throttle-pedal and footbrake, and now I was trying to get my gear without operating the clutch. Needless to say, the bogey time for the test had elapsed long before ever I got the car into motion.

Composure was regained slightly after a successful non-stop climb of Nailsworth Ladder, because " The Ladder," which runs up from just outside Nailsworth directly on to Rodborough Common, and is steep, with a very rough surface of rock outcrop, had quite a reputation. The " Abingdon," however, was being run during a spell of fine dry weather, when the rocky type of surface loses its slipperiness. The weather had also taken the sting out of the remainder of the non-stop hills included in the route, Mutton, Quarhouse, Iles Lane, and Battlescombe, and I was able to make the required performance on all of them. In consequence I did not come home from this first trial completely empty handed. Having failed in only one of the tests to which I had subjected my car and myself, I was entitled to a second-class award.

Better was to follow, almost at once. A week later, in another " short " trial in Derbyshire, with the start and finish at the spa town of Buxton, I got my first " first-class award." That means, of course, that I made the required performance on all of the hills scheduled to be climbed non-stop, and was within bogey time on the re-start. Reverting back to my earlier explanation of the method used for determining the winner, or the driver making the best performance of the day, I did not win this event because other drivers also climbed all the non-stop hills, managed the re-start, and several of them were faster than I was in the special or " against-the-watch " test.

Another success followed when I made a first trip into the Chilterns, another favourite area for clubs organizing half-day trials, and slid round the Chiltern chalk to make third-best performance of the day.

Then the set-backs started. First symptoms of a subsequently most persistent " flat-spot " in the " pick-up " of the engine put me outside bogey time for the stop-and-go test in Sunbac's

" Shell Cup " Trial, and over an unhappy trip into Wales and an unfortunate night trial in the Midlands I prefer to draw a merciful veil. Out of these events, coupled with the fact that the M.G.'s engine continued to " fluff," arose the conviction that I was not yet sufficiently experienced to compete in the two long-distance winter classics, the North-West London Motor Club's London–Gloucester Trial and the Motor Cycling Club's London–Exeter Trial.

Through the winter months, therefore, I followed the sport " on paper," through the columns of those leading, popular, weekly motoring journals, *The Autocar*, *The Motor*, and *The Light Car*. I particularly remember reading, with tremendous interest, how only eighteen of the very large number of competitors in the " London–Exeter " succeeded in making non-stop climbs of a very difficult new hill called Simms, lying just outside the little village of Ilsington in South-East Devon.

CHAPTER II

1934

EARLY in the new year, after the " fluffing " had been finally ironed out by the service specialists of the S.U. Carburettor concern, I decided to have the engine compression-ratio raised by having the cylinder-head machined. I had been advised, by leading drivers, that this modification would result in the engine producing that extra bit of " urge " that was almost essential for the successful surmounting of obstacles like Simms Hill.

The work was entrusted to Messrs. P. J. Evans Ltd., who at that time enjoyed the agency for M.G. cars in Birmingham, although it was not they who would undertake the actual machining, this part of the job being put out to specialists, while " P. J.'s " did all the stripping and refitting.

The first event in which I proposed to compete with the car after the modification had been effected was the trial for the Colmore Trophy, organized by Sunbac. Now, somehow or other, the work of modifying the M.G.'s engine did not get put in hand until about a fortnight before the date of the Colmore Trial. Even so, plenty of time would have been available for the necessary work to be completed if something had not gone wrong.

It was with pleasurable anticipation that, on the Friday after-noon, eight days before the trial, I picked up the telephone and was told : " P. J. Evans for you, Mr. May. Mr. Elwell, service department, wants you." We were connected, but although the voice that came through from the other end of the wire was familiar, the tone of that voice boded ill. All that was said was : " We have just got your cylinder-head back ; can you come down and see it?"—but the manner of saying it sounded ominous. I went.

One glance at the cylinder-head was sufficient to show that a real bodge job had been made of the machining, for all that it had been carried out by a reputable firm of long standing, to whom Messrs. P. J. Evans Ltd. regularly entrusted this type of work. " P. J.'s " were worried and apologetic ; they felt a responsibility as having recommended the particular firm which had carried out the machining ; I was livid ; the reputable firm of long standing was curiously and persistently unhelpful.

No measuring instruments were required to show that the cylinder-head had been rendered unfit for further service ; the damage done was obvious to the naked eye. It had been my intention to join company, on the Sunday, with a number of other drivers who would be competing in the forthcoming Colmore Trial, to make a sort of " rehearsal " run on some of the hills which it was popularly supposed would be included in the route. Obviously that outing was now out of the question : there was doubt, even, about getting the car running again for the trial itself, the next Saturday. That doubt was set at rest, however, after a trunk call to the M.G. factory had elicited a ready promise to have another cylinder-head, not machined, of course, dispatched at once.

In point of fact I did join the party on the Sunday " rehearsal " run, through the kindness of an enthusiast of the fair sex, Miss Olive Bailey, who generously offered to squash me into the back of her Sports Singer Nine. That I caught a chill in the process was not her fault : one sat pretty high in the rear of those first open-bodied Sports Singers, and this was the middle of February. But I did not let my cold keep me in when, on Wednesday morning, there came the message I had expected to receive the previous Friday, that the M.G. was ready for the road again.

The " Colmore " struck a novel note by having the start of the route sited directly at the foot of the first non-stop section, Gypsy Lane, near Winchcombe. Gypsy has no exceptional gradient and is of the type which relies almost entirely upon the nature of its surface to create difficulty for the competitor. The hill is, or was at that time, used normally only for horse-drawn traffic, so that the surface was comprised of deep, irregular ruts, thickly coated with mud and wet clay.

One hundred and fifty-seven competitors set out on the 1934 Colmore Trophy Trial, on Saturday, February 24th, and, as it happened, I was first man away, the others following on at the usual one-minute intervals.

I shot into the mud and ruts of Gypsy Lane " flat-out " in first gear, the M.G. really doing its stuff. The little car slewed from side to side, " crabbed " at frightening angles, and all but ran out of control, the steering being almost unmanageable in the criss-crossed, deep ruts. I decided to " soft-pedal " a bit, and it proved a right decision, the car maintaining sufficient " way " to plough through the mud, but answering to the steering wheel sufficiently for it to be kept from skidding off the narrow, slimy track.

Mill Lane came next, and here, as in the " Abingdon " the previous autumn, a stop-and-go test was to be undertaken, but with the engine kept running, as was the more usual method. These tests were still very much my *bête noire*, but my performance this time exceeded my most sanguine hopes, and I learned afterwards that I was well within bogey time. On Old Stanway hill —not, of course, the main road hill of that name, but a rough-surfaced, fairly steep, disused lane, branching off the main road just where that road swings sharply to the right—was staged the special test. From a standing-start cars had to accelerate over 20 yards, stop with the front wheels inside an area about 4 feet long, and, on the dropping of a flag by an official of the organizing club, accelerate over another 20 yards, and again stop with the front wheels inside a 4-foot area—actually a sort of double stop-and-go test. This, too, I managed to cope with fairly satisfactorily : certainly all the right knobs, pedals, and levers were pressed at the right moments, even if the over-all time was not brilliant.

Kineton hill, which came next, was not difficult. This was fortunate for me, because I made the classic error of the inexperienced driver, that of not giving the engine enough " revs " on the take-off from the standing-start, so that there were a few anxious moments while the engine got into its stride.

Some more or less main-road work followed and led eventually to the Royal George Hotel, near Birdlip. At this point roughly half the course had been covered. I was delighted with the way my car was running, but several stiff obstacles still lay before us.

The next test, to quote *The Autocar* of March 2nd, 1934, "was held up in those wonderful hills close to Stroud, and consisted of an acceleration test up a steep grade, over about 70 yards, with a right-hand hairpin corner and a left-hand curve. At the end of the distance the cars had to come to a stop inside a distance of 20 yards, and then carry on. The surface was loose on the top and firm beneath, and the gradient sufficiently steep to need bottom gear."

The term for this style of test, in the trials jargon, is " timed climb," there being a bogey time for the test just as in a stop-and-go test. The site of this timed climb in the 1934 " Colmore " was a hill called Stancombe.

Again my M.G. did its stuff and repeated the performance, a few miles farther on, at Station Lane, Chalford. I had not seen this hill before, and it proved to be a long, narrow lane, with a bumpy, rocky surface, inclined to be slimy, but not particularly severe as to gradient.

I had a shock at Nailsworth Ladder, next non-stop hill on the route. " The Ladder," in 1934, was regarded as one of the more difficult of the regularly used hills, but Sunbac had stepped up its difficulties by setting a stop-and-go test at the foot of the hill, the non-stop section following immediately from this stop-and-go test, so that the starting-line for the stop-and-go test formed also the starting-point for the climb of the non-stop section.

Here was a case where I really gained from the fitting of the lower-ratio crown-wheel and bevel-pinion, and would have felt the benefit also of the higher engine compression-ratio, had that modification been successfully carried out in time for this trial, as I had hoped. The lower gears enabled me to get my " revs " more quickly, and, as I remembered this time to bang the throttle really wide open before I eased in the clutch upon receiving the " go " signal in the stop-and-go test, I got within bogey time for the test, and pulled through the non-stop section above also.

Only one more test was still to be undertaken, a non-stop climb of Ham Mill. Ham Mill rises steeply from the Chalford valley on to Rodborough Common, terminating close to the well-known Bear Hotel. This also was a hill I had not seen previously. It had a surface mainly of rock, with a lot of big, loose stones lying about, and was, in places, terribly rough. But I was not to be so unfortunate as to fall at the last hurdle, and the little M.G. bucketed its way to the top non-stop.

Well, that was my first big trial in 1934, and from then onwards I drove regularly in trial after trial. Some folk, whom I hope will be reading this book, may feel that I have gone to un-necessary detail with my description of the 1934 " Colmore." They will be the people who have had direct contact with trials, and who can immediately draw up a mind-picture of Ham Mill or " The Ladder," merely from the name, without requiring any further description of the nature of the hill. But I know that there are a lot of other people who have not had physical contact with trials, but are still enthusiastic motorists, and may I hope, be reading the book in consequence, who find the exact nature of our sport a bit puzzling.

I hope, however, that the less initiated will have got a " line " on the trials game at this stage, and I want now to introduce some of the leading figures of the sport, the men who, by their regular and enthusiastic support of trials, kept the sport alive and healthy.

The best performance of the day in the " Colmore " was recorded by R. A. Macdermid with a J2 M.G. Winner of the Bernard Norris Cup for best performance by a car with an engine of more than 1100 c.c. was J. A. M. Patrick. Patrick, well-known Birmingham motor agent, was driving one of the bigger Sports Singers, with the 1496 c.c. six-cylinder engine, a type of car featuring very prominently in the trials of the day.

Three such cars, one painted red, one white, one blue, appeared in almost every event, driven by J. D. Barnes, J. R. H. Baker, and A. H. (Alfred) Langley, all of whom I had got to know. Barnes, together with his brother, F. S., had had racing experience, having competed in the Tourist Trophy races on the Ards circuit, in Ulster, and at Brooklands, usually with the racing type Austin Sevens.

Baker, who practised law, had his home at Stratford on Avon, of which town he later became mayor two years in succession. Langley, brother to A. B. Langley mentioned earlier, was a Birmingham man, though of Yorkshire extraction.

Austin fortunes in trials at this period were in the hands, for the most part, of J. G. Orford, prominent member of Sunbac and one of the first drivers to take the little Austins into competition, R. J. Richardson, another Birmingham man, and W. J. Milton from London.

A. B. Langley, of whom I wrote earlier on as an M.G. exponent, had since " swapped horses," and was now driving one of the attractive looking, new two-seater Le Mans model Singer Nines, forming a regular trio with H. M. Avery, already mentioned, and W. J. B. Richardson, a London man and a driver of extensive experience. Also from London and fast becoming a leading light in the Singer " camp " was M. H. Lawson, whose name will appear frequently in this book.

I was, as might be expected, a member of the M.G. Car Club

as well as of Sunbac. The popularity of the M.G. car was caus-
ing the c lub to expand at such a rate that separate, self-contained
centres of the club were being established, one such coming into
being in the Midlands. I became associated even more closely
with the activities of this organization than with those of Sunbac,
and built up a close personal friendship with the secretary,
J. F. Kemp.

Of those 157 drivers who set out to tackle the " Colmore,"
only 19 finished " clean " (*i.e.* without fault). One of them was
Crawford, driving a new model Wolseley Hornet Special. Another was W. H. Haden, a Cheltenham dental surgeon, with
whom Crawford and I struck up a personal friendship, and
later, as will be described, the three of us formed a team to have
a " crack " at the Team Award, which was invariably put up
for competition in the leading events. Bastock, with his J2
model M.G., was another of the 19, and so was Avery. Another
driver successful in the " Colmore " was K. Hutchison, who will
be met many times in this story of the trials days. He was one
of the drivers who still preferred the bigger type of car, competing
with a Ford V8.

Less successful in this particular event, but to appear just as
frequently in the course of this narrative, was N. V. Terry, a
director of Herbert Terry Ltd., the well-known spring specialists,
at Redditch. Terry, who at this time was driving one of the
T.T. replica, 1496 c.c. Frazer-Nashes, and myself became close
friends. I also knew well M. G. Billingham, who, a month or so
later, turned up to a trial in full morning dress and top-hat on a
day of scorching sunshine, his passenger similarly dressed. They
had rushed straight to the start from a wedding reception, and
I always remember the occasion. Billingham started in trials
much about the same time as myself, at first driving one of the
Sports Singer Nines with the coupé body, but later appearing
with what, on external appearance, was a standard " family
saloon " model Singer. On investigation this proved to have
the sports engine and gear-box fitted.

Another Birmingham driver, still in the early stages like
myself, was J. H. Summerfield. Summerfield had purchased
one of the first of the long-chassis, full four-seater bodied, model
" K " M.G. Magnettes, and had found it to be, at any rate for
trials' purposes, under-engined and over-bodied. He overcame
the problem by having a big supercharger fitted to the engine,

and he must have been one of the first to make use of this device for trials' purposes ; " blowers," as we called the supercharger unit, being a device for boosting power output more usually found on the out-and-out racing machine.

One often met wives, sweethearts, and girl friends in the passenger's seat, or observing on the non-stop hills and at special tests, but it was the exception to see them at the wheel. I knew personally one member of the alleged weaker sex who was building up something of a reputation in motor sport, and was no doubt destined to go a long way if ill health had not forced her to give up driving, and that was Miss " Jackie " Astbury.

The 1934 London–Land's End Trial created a record in that more cars were entered (366 in all) than had been the case in any reliability or sporting trial ever held in the history of motor sport. Crawford and myself were among the 366, myself, of course, at the wheel instead of in the capacity of passenger this time.

Both of us enjoyed a trouble-free run of particular enjoyment in weather more reminiscent of midsummer than an early Easter, so that in the Devon and Cornwall lanes there were clouds of thick white dust which settled over car and crew until all were the same colour.

The M.G. Car Co. Ltd. had superseded the J2 model M.G. Midget with a new job to be known as the " P " type. The new car still employed the 847 c.c., 8 h.p. engine, and was fitted with much the same style of two-seater sports bodywork as the J2, and might be summed up in a few simple words as a refined and sturdier version of the J2 model. Macdermid was driving one in the " Land's End," and I endeavoured to compare notes with him during the short halt at Willoughby Hedge. Macdermid did not seem over-enamoured of the new model, and remarked simply that it went well on the flat, but when the results were published I saw that he had succeeded in making a climb of every one of the non-stop hills, most of which were very far from flat !

It so happened that the day after the trial, running up from St. Ives, where my passenger and myself had stayed the night, to Exeter, I fell in with one of the " P " type M.G.s, which, from the evidence of the two spare wheels shod with competition tyres, had been through the trial, and we had a friendly " scrap " for miles. There seemed to be nothing in it for performance.

I was hurrying to Exeter to arrive in time for a luncheon

which was being given at the Rougemont Hotel there by the
M.G. Car Club.   Towards the end of the meal a fellow stood up
and without the slightest preamble announced : " I'm your new
secretary, chaps.   Better have a good look at me."

That was my first introduction to that sportsman journalist,
many years editor of *The Light Car*, F. L. M. Harris.   There can
be few in the motor game who have not, at some time or another,
contacted " Mit " Harris and experienced his terrific and un-
failing sense of humour and extreme charm of manner.   Harris
also edited *The Caravan*, a hobby of which he was passionately
fond ; and later launched a monthly journal for the sportsman,
The Sports Car, mention of, and extracts from which, will appear
often in these pages.

I remember speaking to Harris about a road-test report he
had done for a certain magazine.   He said he was glad that I
liked it and perhaps I could tell him something about the car,
because he himself had never ridden in one of the wretched
things, having concocted the road test by suitably watering
down the manufacturers' own rather rosy claims of performance
appearing in their advertising matter—probably quite untrue,
but a sample of the Harris humour.

Although the " Land's End " had gone off so well for me,
the M.G. seemed very " tired " after it, and the engine was using
quite a drop of oil, while the clutch tended to run hot.   Then,
the very day before the next event in which I was proposing to
compete—the " Abingdon–Abingdon," brought forward from
September to April for the 1934 event—several piston-rings
broke.

Now it happened that opposite to my business premises was
the Birmingham depôt of a Cheltenham firm of motor dealers,
with whom I was very friendly.   The head mechanic there,
hearing of my eleventh-hour trouble, said he felt sure he could
manage to draw the pistons, fit new rings where found necessary,
and reassemble in the short time available ; and I let him try.
He was as good as his word, and the car was on the road again
in the evening.   But I went off to the start, which was again to
take place from the M.G. factory at Abingdon, thoroughly out
of sorts.   I don't like new " bits " in the engine at the very last
minute, with the journey from your home to the start the sole
means of running them in before asking the engine for its maximum output again.   It rained, too, on the way down.

At the foot of every non-stop hill I said to myself that this was where we should " blow-up," but " we " didn't, and, what is more, the M.G. went on to make the best performance of the day, and I collected my first trophy. Then, of all things, when the report of the event appeared later in *The M.G. Magazine*, an accompanying photograph was stated to be of me, yet it depicted a " P " type M.G., driven by a man in a white linen racing helmet : and that you must not wear a white helmet under any conditions was one of the very first things I learned about trials ! Not that I ever wanted to wear one ; I am a founder member of the no-hat brigade.

I was so sure that the car was at breaking-point at the end of the trial (I did not know straightaway that I had made the best performance of the day) that when I discovered an alternative method of getting back to my home in Birmingham I left my car at the factory. W. E. C. Watkinson, who had won the University Motors Trophy (for best performance of the day over 1100 c.c.) in the previous year's Abingdon Trial, had his four-seater Speed 20 Alvis there, and was going through to Malvern, where my mother was staying at the time, and she had her car with her. So my passenger and I went with Watkinson, at his kind invitation, burst in on my mother, to her considerable surprise, and " pinched " her car to complete our journey to Birmingham.

I got my car back at the end of the following week, all washed, pressed, and brushed up ready for the London–Edinburgh run at Whitsun.

The car used regularly for trials and competition work would usually be found to have additions to, and modifications of, the manufacturer's standard range of equipment. My own car was no exception to this rule. After fitting one of the popular and sensibly designed spring-spoked steering-wheels, " quick-lift," or " racing pattern " filler-caps to radiator and petrol tank, in addition, of course, to carrying the inevitable two spare wheels shod with competition tyres, and a plate back and front to which to fix competition numbers, I changed the slow-acting, suction-type windscreen wiper for an electrically operated one, and then decided to have the instrument panel re-equipped.

I expect you remember the instrument panel layout of the old J2 model Midgets, a large-dial speedometer, calibrated also to show the equivalent engine revolutions in top and third gears, was set before the driver, and balanced on the passenger's side by a panel combining the oil-pressure gauge, the ammeter, the light and ignition switches, and the ignition " tell-tale." In the centre of the board were the horn-button, dipper-switch, and rear-view mirror. I replaced the speedometer with a revolution counter, the camshaft, from which the drive for the instrument was to be taken, being already drilled and tapped for the purpose, and placed the speedometer in front of the passenger. The oil-pressure gauge, ammeter, etc., were set separately either side of the centrally placed horn-button, and there was added a thermometer to show the temperature of the radiator water, the radiator header-tank ready tapped for such a fitting, as was the camshaft for the revolution counter drive, and a clock.

The panel itself, which was of mottled aluminium and tended to set up glare, was cellulosed dark green, to match the car's mudguards, at the end of which I felt that the car had acquired quite a " personality."

Going to my home from business on the Friday afternoon, in order to pack my bag and change my clothes before setting out down to Wrotham Park, Barnet, to start in the London–Edinburgh Trial, I experienced what appeared to be sudden, wild clutch slip. Cold shivers ran down my back. Agitatedly I checked the adjusting toggles and carefully checked the amount of " free " movement. Perhaps I had been mistaken, perhaps it had been violent wheelspin on smooth, wet tramline, but I ought to be able to distinguish between the two by now. I changed, packed, started back to town to pick up my passenger. This was no wheelspin ! I collected the passenger, we went round a couple of blocks, staged a practice stop-and-go test on a bit of steep but metalled-surfaced road, and it was obviously hopeless. I rang up Crawford, with whom I had arranged to run in company again. He wanted me to try to struggle through. The passenger was not keen ; neither was I. We didn't go.

Just as suddenly the luck changed. I achieved four good runs in successive week-ends, in the Brighton and Hove Motor Club's Brighton–Beer Trial (which had neither started at Brighton nor finished at Beer for some time, but the name was retained for traditional reasons), the Liverpool Motor Club's £100 Trial in North Wales (one of the very few events in which an actual cash award was offered—I did not win it), Sunbac's Trial for the Vesey Cup, and the Motor Cycling Club's Summer Trial, finishing at Llandudno.

Each brought its mede of adventure, excitement, and unusual experience. The most embarrassing moment was at the start of the trial to Llandudno when I discovered that I had left my wallet at home and had with me only small change amounting to less than £1, so that I had to be rescued by that " grand old man " of the sport, S. H. Roe. Best performance of the day at Llandudno was recorded by Singer driver M. H. Lawson.

For the " Vesey," Sunbac had obtained the use of private parkland on Enville Common, near Stourbridge. Here a section was included of the " farthest-up-wins " type, since it was not anticipated that any car would get to the top of the section, which was nothing but a very steep footpath, rising very suddenly, with a surface (!) of beaten earth plentifully studded with tree roots.

Summerfield was competing with the supercharged M.G., and shot straight over the top at some velocity, spectators scattering hastily. In point of fact, there was no way out at the top, and Summerfield found himself faced by a most substantial looking hedge, with precious little room in which to pull up ! However, the hedge was not demolished, Summerfield achieving a " phenomenal avoidance."

The Mid-Surrey Automobile Club's London–Barnstaple Trial ranked as one of the classics. It was always staged at the August Bank Holiday week-end, starting on the Friday night. For the 1934 event the night section, from London to Minehead, was made optional, and the following year was dropped entirely, the trial starting from Minehead on the Saturday morning.

I decided not to do the night section, and travelled down to Minehead on the Friday evening, to start from there first thing on Saturday morning. *En route* a front tyre punctured. Not wishing to bring one of the competition-tyred spare wheels into use at the front if it could be avoided, the passenger and I endeavoured to get the puncture mended. Considerable delay ensued before we got under way again, so that it was already getting dark when we reached Glastonbury, whereas, originally, we had planned to be in Minehead for the evening meal.

When we did arrive, tired and late, we arranged for a call in the morning, lest we overslept. The call did not come, we did oversleep, and there was a mad rush to make the start on time, not helped by the fact of another car being parked across the exit from the garage in which the M.G. had been placed overnight, and proving most difficult to move.

I was, in consequence, still a little hot and bothered when I arrived at Lyn Hill, just outside Lynton. The principal difficulty is a very sharp right-hand hairpin corner near the foot. I came into this corner, which I was seeing for the first time, much too fast, and was unable to get round. As the hairpin was in the non-stop section, I registered failure.

Thereafter I went off for a short holiday. I joined some friends on a week's sea cruise to Hamburg. The ship docked back at Liverpool at the end of the trip on a Saturday morning, and that same evening I was setting out, in the M.G., for Bournemouth, to compete in the West Hants Club's first trial for the Knott Trophy.

On the run down, even before reaching Stratford on Avon from Birmingham, the bolt sheared that used to hold the front mudguard to its support-bracket at its upper end. I jury-rigged with wire and rope and hoped to get fixed up with a new bolt at the M.G. Garages in Oxford. Between Enstone and Woodstock the clutch started to slip. Having got up early that morning and had a tiring train journey down from Liverpool to Birmingham, with only a " cat-nap " since, I was of two minds whether to go on. It started to rain a little also. Finally, I decided to continue, and in Oxford a new mudguard support bolt was obtained and fitted. But beyond Winchester—it was now dark—I missed my way, and in the New Forest, racing to make Bournemouth on time, the M.G. was all but upset in a wild, wicked slide on a corner badly misjudged in the darkness. Within a few yards of the start a front tyre punctured. Oh ! it was quite a " party."

The night section, as was customary, was mostly on main roads, and led to Taunton. From there the route went on down the Exe valley, and, in the early dawn, came to the first non-stop hill, Hatherland, near Dulverton. Hatherland had first been used in the previous year's Brighton–Beer Trial, and had stopped almost the entire entry. In the current season's Brighton–Beer Trial the hill had not proved anything like so difficult, but the 1934 " Beer " had been run in weather that really justified the old tag, " flaming " June.

For the " Knott " the hill was wet again, and, in no way assisted by another bout of clutch slip, I failed. But I failed in good company, since only two drivers, though both were in M.G. Midgets like mine, managed to make non-stop climbs.

They were A. E. Hann and J. E. S. Jones. Jones, who owned a flour-mill at Bruton, in Somerset, will be met frequently in these pages. He went on to win the Knott Cup.

I then tried my hand at another form of motor sport. Once a year the Motor Cycling Club, sponsors of the " Land's End," the " Edinburgh," and the " Exeter," used to stage a meeting at Brooklands for club members only, driving their trials and road cars. This opportunity for a " spot of speed " was eagerly seized upon by many of the regular trials drivers. The principal event at these meetings was the One-Hour Run, wherein drivers ran on the track continuously for an hour, piling up in the time as much mileage as they desired, or thought their cars capable of achieving without stress.

Perhaps you have competed at one of these meetings ? If so, you must surely be thinking of those terrific mass starts from the Fork, and imagining yourself again, sitting in your car amongst forty or fifty other machines of every size, make, and colour, all about to rush off together in one howling bunch at the fall of " Ebby's " (A. V. Ebblewhite, the official timekeeper) flag— although it will not be Ebby next time, since he has passed on.

For me, who had never attained to real racing, those mass starts remain as one of my more exciting competition memories.

After Brooklands, another new experience, but this time an unfortunate one, my first mechanical breakdown *en route*. In the Light Car Club's Buxton–Buxton Trial the M.G. disconcertingly stripped the teeth on the crown-wheel and bevel-pinion. The car was towed back into Buxton by a breakdown truck, and, just when I had resigned myself to abandoning the car to the care of the local garage, not at all looking forward to the involved and wearying train journey which would be necessary to fetch the car when it was ready for the road again, Alan Hunt offered to tow me home to Birmingham behind his " P " type M.G.

I did not remember having met Hunt before on trials, but he knew me, and I discovered that he had driven in a number of the same events in which I had been competing, the " Beer," the " Vesey," and the " Barnstaple " among others. Now I had never had occasion to be towed before, and, believe me, there is quite an art both in towing and being towed. Hunt and myself learned a good deal about it that afternoon, and we were thankful, indeed, that it was a fine afternoon.

I tackled another trial in the Buxton area, the Motor Cycling

Club's One-Day Sporting Trial. All of the hills, except one, were those with which I had now become fairly familiar, after competing in several events in this area. The new non-stop hill included in the route of the 1934 One-Day Sporting Trial was Bamford Clough.

Bamford Clough is dead straight, and cuts a very closely packed bunch of contour lines at right-angles, and, at the time of its introduction into trials, was undoubtedly the most consistently steep hill which competitors had, up to that time, attempted to climb non-stop. I said, in the beginning of this book, that sheer gradient alone, without, also, the addition of a bad surface, rarely stopped the trials car at this stage. Bamford, at any rate at the first time of asking, was one of the rare occasions, since the surface, though not metalled, was not bad judged by the trials driver's standards. Actually it was a combination of gradient with LENGTH, rather than surface, that made Bamford Clough such a " terror."

My car went up Bamford non-stop, but only just ; another few yards of gradient would have brought it to a standstill. I do not think that any of the more heavily bodied " P " type Midgets got up. Crawford was successful with the Hornet Special, and so was Terry with the Frazer-Nash, but unfortunately both had stopped elsewhere. W. J. B. Richardson, leading the Le Mans Singer Nine team, was successful at Bamford and also on all of the other non-stop hills, and so was J. G. Orford with the Sports Austin Seven. Only 12 competitors out of the 150 who started were " clean " all round. I had come to a stop on the loose stones of Blackermill, so that my climb of Bamford was nullified.

CHAPTER III

Uphill Work

RIGHT after that a lot of things all happened at once. The M.G. Car Club, in line with many of the leading motoring organizations, used to stage a dinner-dance every year during the period of the Motor Show, the venue being the Park Lane Hotel. A certain number of drivers who had been prominent in competition during the season used to receive invitations from the club to this dinner-dance, and be the guests of the club during the function. To my great delight, and even greater surprise, I received an invitation, which I lost no time in accepting.

Now I had been toying with the idea of changing my J2 model M.G. for one of the newer " P " type cars. Macdermid was doing all right with his, even if he did still insist that " it went well on the flat," and those two other leading M.G. exponents, Jack Bastock and J. Maurice Toulmin, had also changed over from the J2 model to the " P " type. I was attracted by an advertisement of Messrs. Jarvis Ltd., the M.G. agents out at Wimbledon, offering a nearly new " P " type, " showroom " condition and with full *de luxe* equipment.

I made arrangements to go straight through to Wimbledon from my home in Birmingham, in the morning, to consider a part-exchange deal on my J2 and the " P " type, put in a quick visit to the Motor Show in the afternoon, and carry on to the dinner-dance in the evening. On top of that Summerfield rang me up, stuck for a passenger for the North-West London Motor Club's inter-team trial in North Devon, starting from Hartland on the Saturday morning (the dinner-dance was on the Thursday evening). It sounded rather a big programme to carry through, but I decided to " have a go."

I liked the look of the " P " type M.G. at Jarvis's ; the paint-work and general external condition were excellent, and seemed to bear out the very low mileage which was all the car was reputed to have done since first being taxed and put on the road. The full range of *de luxe* equipment was there all right : oil- and water-thermometers, a clock, and a grab-handle on the instrument panel ; hinge-up type headlamp stone-guards, quick-lift filler caps, even a bonnet strap (although this I quickly discarded, feeling it to come in the " white helmet " category). Messrs. Jarvis and myself came to terms, and I drove back into London on the " P " type, albeit reluctant to say a final good-bye to the well-tried J2, with which I had experienced so much fun and adventure.

Like most forms of organized recreation, motor sport had a strong social side. I had already sampled it in varying degrees : indeed, the informal dinner and film show at the Palace Hotel at Buxton, following the One-Day Sporting Trial, was still very fresh in my mind. But the M.G. show-time dinner-dance at the Park Lane Hotel proved the absolute highlight.

Lord Nuffield himself was in the chair, ably supported by Mr. Cecil Kimber, managing director of the M.G. Car Co. Ltd. To my further great delight, towards the end of the dinner Lord Nuffield personally made a small presentation to each of us who were there by invitation, about thirty of us in all. It took the form of an ash-tray embodying the M.G. octagon motif, and inscribed : " To C. A. N. May as a token of appreciation from Lord Nuffield, Oct. 1934." I felt that was, indeed, a grand climax to my first full season in motor sport.

I did not know then, of course, that the ensuing twelve months would constitute something of a let-down, and that I should come to the next show-time dinner-dance, not on the " P " type Midget which I had bought that day, but on an " N " Magnette.

But that is anticipating. I kept my date with Summerfield, and went along in the rôle of passenger in the inter-team trial. He, too, now had one of the " P " type Midgets, but the performance had been greatly enhanced by the fitting of a big supercharger to the engine.

The run down to North Devon on the Friday evening—the start of the trial being fixed for early on the Saturday morning—was enlivened when, south of Bristol, along those fast, straight stretches towards Bridgwater, Summerfield caught up with Patrick, driving his white, 1½-litre Singer. He was polling along at around the 75-80 m.p.h. mark, and was momentarily surprised when he suddenly realized that another car was overtaking him at that speed, his first thought being " Police ! "

Summerfield managed to draw alongside and, as I tried to shout across and make myself heard above the combined exhaust noises and the wind roar, Patrick realized who we were, and we pulled up and had a few minutes' chat. Patrick took the lead when we resumed, but, after a few miles, we found that the M.G. was overhauling the Singer on every bit of uphill road. Beyond Bridgwater the Singer got slower and slower, until finally Patrick pulled up under a street-lamp on the outskirts of Minehead, to find what he had feared—that the drive to the distributor was breaking up, a trouble previously experienced. He decided to struggle on, and Summerfield tailed behind him, but the ascent of Porlock hill was painful, and the Singer gasped its last at Lynmouth. It was now late, and Summerfield decided to " call it a day " there also, arranging to be called early enough to complete the run through to Hartland first thing in the morning.

After taking a sad leave of Patrick and his passenger, faced with a dreary all-day bus and train journey to get back to Birmingham, we had to use all of the " blown " Midget's per-formance to get through to Hatherland in time in the morning. A very strong head wind was blowing.

This was an event for teams instead of individual performance, and the regulations provided for each team to comprise four cars, of which the three best performances would count. Summerfield had been asked to run as fourth man to the Toulmin-Bastock-Macdermid M.G. trio.

For me the event opened up a new corner of North Devon, although the first hill on the route, Darracott, was familiar as having featured in the " Land's End " route. Now, however, it was used as the venue for a " timed climb," instead of a straight-forward non-stop hill, the timed section including the three hairpin corners which form the feature of this hill, a most exciting business. Hackmarsh, taken next, was sticky, but in the stop-and-go test at Mineshop only one competitor in the whole entry managed to get inside the bogey time, and that was Maurice Toulmin on his " P " type M.G. Midget. When, a couple of years later, the Motor Cycling Club introduced a new non-stop hill into the route of the " Land's End " and called it Crackington, this proved to be none other than Mineshop under a new name.

I thought that Hartland Quay, where the trial finished, was about the last place on earth, but maybe it looks different when the sun is shining. The outing was capped with success when the results showed *The Sporting Life* Trophy, the award for best performance, to have been won by the team of Toulmin, Bastock, and Summerfield.

Now, about BPH 418, my " P " type M.G. Midget. The extra solidity and refinement of the " P " type, over and above the earlier J2 model, had been obtained at the cost of a noticeable increase in weight, which was not offset by any perceptible increase in the power output of the engine. No great drawback for main road motoring, but definitely bad for the increasingly difficult conditions being provided by trials organizers.

In seeking a cure, the path of least resistance was first taken, a crown-wheel and bevel-pinion being inserted that provided a lower set of gear-ratios. Unfortunately, the transmission proved unequal to the strain imposed upon it, and, in a period of ten months, five crown-wheels broke up. One of these breakages set me on the road to friendship with that leading motor sportsman and consistently successful competition driver, Guy Warburton.

It happened on Wool Heath, Dorsetshire, during the Great West Motor Club's trial for their Spring Cup, the club having obtained permission to use certain sections on war department land at Bovington Camp. On this area, normally used for army manœuvres, it was possible to provide non-stop hills with very " sudden " gradients and surfaces (!) of loose sand. The crown-wheel stripped its teeth right in the centre of the heath, and how Warburton, whom I knew by name, but did not recollect having met previously in person, discovered my plight, I never quite knew, but he appeared suddenly " out of the blue," and suggested towing my car into Bournemouth.

Warburton, like Hutchison, mentioned earlier, had not succumbed to the popular fashion for using the small, high-performance little sports cars in competition, and pinned his faith to a " 30/98 " Vauxhall, with open four-seater bodywork. I was delighted, and Warburton set off to Bournemouth at incredible speed, the old Vauxhall making no more bones about towing the M.G. than if it had had a balloon on a piece of string behind it.

The other side of the picture was when the breakage occurred on Park Rash hill in the early hours of the morning, during the 1935 London–Edinburgh run. Knowing that the car could not be shifted off the hillside until all the following competitors had gone by, the passenger and myself tried to open up the axle casing on the spot. We made a poor job of it. From a fellow M.G. driver I secured a replacement crown-wheel and pinion, but there remained the job of first removing the broken parts and then fitting in these replacements.

Everything conspired against us. It was a sad story, and I will tell you only that it was early evening before the car was again ready for the road. Then we did the maddest thing. We set out to go the rest of the way to Edinburgh (Park Rash is in Yorkshire), what for I do not know. Maybe by that time we had become a little light headed. We did not go quite so mad as to try to pick up the trials route, and follow that through. We did get across on to the Great North Road, but Heaven alone knows what for. We reached Edinburgh about 10.30 p.m.— and started back home to Birmingham straight after breakfast the next morning !

Even before I went in for the altered gear-ratios, in fact before I ran the car in a competitive event at all, I had the cylinder-head machined, to raise the compression (not, this time, by the reputable firm of long standing), and also had the combustion spaces sprayed with aluminium. Shock-absorbers were a problem on the " P " type. In place of the sturdy, friction type " shockers" standardized on the J2, small hydraulic pattern ones were used on the " P " type. For competition purposes these did not prove strong enough, and were less easy of adjustment than the friction pattern.

However, it was not all depression, that ten months with BPH 418, not by a very long way. Crawford, W. H. Haden, and myself formed ourselves into a regular team. Crawford had bought one of the 1287 c.c., six-cylinder " N " Magnettes. The " N " Magnette was a comparative newcomer in the M.G. range, coming off the production line on April 1st, 1934, when it superseded the earlier " F " and " L " type Magnas. Haden, whose association with M.G. cars went back to the original fabric-bodied " M " type Midgets, was running a " P " type. At the suggestion of Frank Kemp, secretary of the Midland Centre of the M.G. Car Club, we represented that body.

The organized team, usually of three identical cars, frequently painted the same colour and bearing the team name or " colours " on the bonnet sides, was fast becoming a dominating feature in our sport, team rivalry being terrific. Crawford, Haden, and myself did not have three identical cars, nor three cars of the same colour, but we did have a team " emblem." It consisted of the M.G. octagon in cream, edged in brown, with a brown stripe diagonally across the octagon, and was painted on either side of the bonnets just behind the radiators.

The team came up at the first time of asking, which was in the 1934 London–Gloucester trial. " A marathon Gloucester " was the way *The Autocar* described this event. More than 130 cars started out from the Bridge House at Staines, and many drivers both started and finished in the dark, so long were the delays caused by the wholesale failures. All the regular Cotswold " terrors " were used, and there was a new " find," Old Hollow, which proved tremendously difficult, so that only four competitors came through to the finish without penalty—Crawford, Haden, H. M. Avery, and Miss Phyllis Goodban (Singer Nine). My car failed on Nailsworth Ladder, so that it was to Crawford and Haden went the credit for our first team success.

The team was successful also in the M.G. Car Club's 1935 Chilterns Trial, and again in the same club's Abingdon–Abingdon Trial. Thereafter Crawford was unable to continue with the team. An unhappy accident after the 1935 " Land's End " resulted in a temporary suspension of his driving licence, a harsh verdict, in no way supported by the true facts of the case.

All around me, during that ten months with the " P " type, the trials scene developed apace. Trials organizers were right on their toes, and the spate of new hills introduced in this period was remarkable. The Kershams and Cloutsham enlivened The Experts' Trial, away down on Exmoor ; King John's Lane—an experiment never repeated—nearly wrecked the Singer Motor Car Club's first trial in the Midlands ; Old Hollow wrought havoc in the " Gloucester " ; and a new version of Kineton shook Colmore Trophy Trial competitors. Just outside Buxton, rocky, chassis-twisting Cowlow came into use ; and with the Brighton–Beer Trial came the king of them all—Widlake.

For those readers to whom these are merely names devoid of any meaning I would like to give a word or two of introduction, and for those drivers who know every bump on Widlake I can only suggest that this is an opportunity to skip a page or so.

Many trials hills seemed to lose their difficulties with the passing of the years, but not so Widlake. It runs directly off the main road that winds all down the Exe Valley, from Dunster, right through Timberscombe and Cutcombe, to Dulverton, and eventually down to Exeter. Just before a point known as Coppleham Cross, where the road to the little village of Winsford forks away to the right, Widlake goes straight up the high overhanging bluff, topped with trees, that is on the left-hand side of the main road. It is steep, narrow, and overhanging trees shut in the track for almost all of its length. The surface is mainly of slippery rock slab, so irregular as to form actual steps at several points, and has several deep cross gullies, the whole thing finishing up in a farmyard, to which it is said to be the sole means of access. Obviously the farmer must rely upon horse-drawn transport, since of the 132 cars which set out in the 1935 Brighton–Beer Trial, into the route for which event this hill was introduced for the first time, three reached the farmyard non-stop, and cars have been spinning to a standstill, with only a few exceptions, on the greasy rock slab of Widlake ever since.

Those three drivers who conquered Widlake were Macdermid, Toulmin, and K. R. W. Shackel, with an oldish M.G. Midget tuned up by M. A. McEvoy. Macdermid ultimately made best performance of the day.

The new version of Kineton was a rocky track under trees, branching off to the right immediately at the foot of the hill generally used for cars, and was entered at rather an awkward angle through a gate. The actual gate itself had been removed, but the massive gate-posts remained, and immediately through the gate the gradient was very sharp and the track extremely narrow, resembling nothing so much as an overgrown ditch of the type dug for carrying away flood water. This Kineton is the little village of only a few houses and a farm in the Cotswolds, above Stanway, not the better-known Warwickshire town.

Old Hollow first appeared in the route of a trial in the London–Gloucester Trial of December 8th, 1934, and lies in the southern Cotswolds, no great way from the town of Dursley. It winds up through a wood, and lies beneath overhanging trees nearly all the way, having a sharp, almost " hairpin," left-hand corner towards the summit, the steepest gradient coming at this point. Old Hollow is a very favourite venue for staging stop-and-go tests, and it was in that manner that it was used in the 1934 " Gloucester," with a non-stop section following immediately from the stop-and-go area, and including the left-hand corner.

Cloutsham, which lies roughly between the foot of Dunkery and Horner Wood, in North Somerset, remote from the nearest village, is a tough-looking hill. There is a deceptive approach to a sharp right-hand corner, and then, immediately above this corner, the gradient stiffens appreciably, and the surface (!) deteriorates into a sea of loose rocks and boulders. The track swings back to the left, and then goes up in a series of rock steps formed at an angle to the track, and with more loose rocks strewn about, a difficult climb and rather hard on the under parts of the car.

Kersham, too, is in North Somerset, and is approached from that main Cutcombe-Dulverton-Exe Valley road by doubling back down a narrow lane at a point known as Wheddon Cross. There is a steep, bumpy, and extremely narrow descent to the foot of the hill, which then rises out of a farmyard, round a sharp right-hand corner, on greasy rock slab, with a good deal of rock outcrop above the corner and a gradient of about 1 in 4.

Cowlow lies immediately off the Buxton-Matlock main road, only a mile or so outside Buxton, and zigzags up a hillside, clearly visible from the main road. There is one very acute right-hand corner, at a point where the track is very narrow, and has a high bank on either side. The surface is terribly rough, and takes away much of the enjoyment of attempting successfully to negotiate the quickly following twists and turns of the track.

There was one other hill which really " hit the headlines " in 1935, and that was Leckhampton, included in the route for the Colmore Trophy Trial. Here is the story of Leckhampton as told by *The Autocar* of even date :

" Frightful rumours had been current all day concerning the severity of the last hill, called in the programme Leckhampton and known locally as the Jinny. This hill turned out to be like at least four Simms Hills rolled into one, slippery surface, 1 in $2\frac{1}{2}$ gradient, and tractor were all there." (*Note :* The tractor, actuating a wire cable, was stationed at the summit for the purpose of hauling up cars unable to climb unassisted, it being quite impossible to manhandle a car to the top.) " Yet Simms is in the heart of desolate Dartmoor, while the Jinny is on the very outskirts of the far-flung town of Cheltenham, leading off the main road.

" Special permission had been obtained for the use of the hill, which is common land, and reserved as a rule for walkers only." (*Note :* It formed the base of a now dismantled wire-rope railway to the quarry at its summit.) " But the police stopped the first cars from ascending, and were only prevailed upon after some delay to allow proceedings to go on. Even with the short, sharp Simms . . . there was, in the recent London–Exeter Trial, a long queue of cars waiting. With the immense length of this new terror, Leckhampton . . . a delay would, in any case, have been inevitable, and apart from the short lane leading to the gradient, there was only one place for the waiting cars—the main Cheltenham-Birdlip road !

" Rapidly this main road became choked as well with a double line of spectators' cars. A policeman strove nobly at the entrance to the narrow lane, but he could not be everywhere at once, and for a time complete chaos reigned. Main-road congestion, too, was inevitable with 'racers climbing a precipice' so near a populous town. . . .

" To add to the difficulties of the situation, or, perhaps, to solve them, the tractor broke down when some twenty-two competitors had tried their ascents, of whom only Haden with his M.G. Midget and Attwood with his Magnette were successful. A massive cog burst asunder, and those who were stuck on the hill—were stuck ! A six-wheeled lorry was next reversed down to pull up a car which had stuck, but the caterpillars of this broke under the unequal strain, and the car pulled the lorry down the hill. That finished it. The hill was abandoned, the cars waiting in the lane had to reverse, and the competing cars lined up in the main road went on their way."

The drivers met the new difficulties in a variety of ways, a favourite first step being an attempt to reduce the weight of the cars. The Bastock-Toulmin-Macdermid M.G.s appeared for the " London–Exeter " (December 1934) stripped and shorn of every ounce of surplus weight. In the process the full-valanced, sweeping mudguards were discarded, and light, racing-pattern blades, on the lines of the J2 models, were substituted, giving the cars a curiously unfinished appearance. The three cars were repainted chocolate and brown, Abingdon's official " colours," and had inscribed on the bonnet sides, for the first time, " Cream Cracker," and it is by this team name that these particular three M.G. cars will be identified from this point onwards.

The three new 1½-litre Sports Singers which Baker, Barnes, and A. H. Langley brought to the 1935 Colmore Trial were also much lighter in weight than previously, and rather sketchy as to bodywork. The engines were set farther back in the chassis than in the 1934 cars, all weight being concentrated to the rear, to aid wheelgrip. All three cars were painted dark green instead of one red, one white, one blue.

M.G.s " pushed the boat out " again, and put into trials (their first appearance was in the 1935 " Land's End ") three of the actual " N " Magnettes which had run in the Tourist Trophy Race, on the Ards circuit in Ulster, the previous autumn. They had new bodies, though, of exactly the same pattern as those fitted on the Midgets, with the big, external petrol tanks and two spare wheels on a vertical bracket behind. At the out-set they were driven by Lewis Welch, Kindell, and Nash (or Hounslow). The first car bore on the bonnet sides the name " Athos," the second " Porthos," and the third " Aramis," the team, as a whole, being known as " The Three Musketeers."

The possibilities of weight reduction having been thoroughly exploited, though not exhausted, more power was sought, and the supercharger, hitherto regarded more as the perquisite of the out-and-out racing car, began to appear more and more on the trials cars. First Centric, and then the firm of Marshall, Drew, demonstrated that an efficient and comparatively reliable unit, at a " commercial " price, was now practicable. Macdermid had one, on the " Cream Cracker " Midget, and Toulmin also. By the autumn of 1935 the era of " low pressure " supercharging had been well and truly inaugurated.

Amongst all these comings and goings, I struggled on, but it must be said that the " P " type Midget, judged, I hasten to add, purely on its suitability for the particular job in hand, proved the least happy of the various cars on which I pursued the trials game. The season had its bright spots, however—the Lawrence Cup Trial, for example.

It was my first " Lawrence," but I remembered the motoring press reports of the previous year's event, and how the North-West London Motor Club had introduced a number of startling sections on W.D. ground at Camberley Heath, with alarming gradients and surfaces of loose shale, fine sand, and earth.

The start, on a gloriously sunny afternoon (May 1935), was from " The East Arms," at Hurley. The event got under way most deceptively, with such well-known and comparatively mild non-stop hills as Shillingridge Wood and Maiden's Grove. But we came, in the fullness of time, to the War Department area.

A first sight of the straight, comparatively short, very steep, and terrifyingly " sudden " gradients was rather shattering. The hills started straight off the level, the gradient being " immediate," just like the initial pull-up of the big switchbacks at the South Shore Fun Fair at Blackpool. They levelled off again at the summit just as suddenly, so that, for a few seconds, at the crest, the front end of the car pointed straight into the sky, and the driver had no idea at all of what might lie beyond the top. There were four sections, of which the last counted as two separate climbs, failure on the first automatically entailing failure on the second, and an optional climb of Red Roads.

The track known as Red Roads was reputed to have a gradient as sharp as 1 in 1, and certainly looked like it. This hill had featured, for some years, in the route of a " tough " motor-cycle trial called the Camberley Scramble.

My " P " type, that day, could do no wrong, and, though most of the radiator water boiled away, the car successfully climbed all but Red Roads. I do not know whether my surprise or my delight reached the higher level. I finished as runner-up to J. H. Summerfield's supercharged " P " type, my car's best performance.

I broadened and ripened my circle of friends and acquaintances. I met, and got to know, some of the " Bristol boys," Keith Steadman and Cecil Evans (who were going to be such Good Samaritans to me when I was to break down in the following Easter's " Land's End "). I picked up fresh trials lore from J. C. G. Bond and W. E. C. Greenleaf, from London, who used to do incredible things with (apparently) standard Morris Minor two-seaters. I gleaned from Bond, however, that there was quite a bit of M.G. in the mechanical specification of his Morris. I remember, particularly, that he had fitted an engine revolution counter to his car. It was of the big dial variety, and, as it was quite impossible to accommodate it on the cramped instrument panel of the Minor, Bond had it clamped to the steering column, so that it was customarily referred to as his soup-plate.

I knew well Mrs. A. E. Moss, redoubtable exponent of the alleged weaker sex, prominent in nearly every event with her white, 1½-litre, six-cylinder Singer. Through my team-mate, Bill Haden, I met R. E. (Bob) Sandland, who managed a garage out in the Black Country. After establishing himself with one of the later pattern four-seater Singer Sports Nines, he joined up with D. E. Harris and H. W. Johnson, both of whom I knew well, to form a trio known as the " Ruddy " team. The name arose, I hasten to add, from the fact that they equipped them-selves with three of the special Le Mans model Singers painted a deep maroon.

I enjoyed the ready humour and quick wit of C. G. Fitt, at first an M.G. enthusiast, but, at this stage, doing terrific stuff with a drop-head Ford V8. I was introduced to, and later, got to know very well indeed, Godfrey Imhof, whose " forceful " methods with his white Singer Le Mans, later supercharged, had quickly drawn attention. I knew F. E. Elgood, who upset all calculations in a world seemingly peopled entirely with M.G. and Singer drivers by winning awards with an oldish 3-litre Bentley.

I had quite a bit to do with C. V. Wells, driving one of the extremely attractive, new sports Rileys, who, later, guided the fortunes of the North-West London Motor Club ; and with A. C. Cookson, M.G. exponent, who so ably directed the Central Motor Institute in the Finchley Road, and worked hard on the General Committee of the M.G. Car Club.

Steadily the circle broadened. I learned that the highly exciting, check sports shirts and " gent.'s natty plus-four suit-ings," which had suddenly started to enliven our little world, belonged to L. J. Onslow-Bartlett. Bartlett came into trials with a green " N " Magnette two-seater. The standard pattern front mudguards had been removed and replaced with the much smaller, lighter J2 Midget type, and frequently the car appeared devoid of windscreen, hood, and spare wheel, all in the interests of weight saving. Bartlett was of the " forceful " type, and was successful almost from his first event.

I remember light-hearted, north country Edgar Wadsworth, always good company at a party, and a shade more successful than the average with his Le Mans Singer. Wadsworth quickly followed the prevailing " fashion " of forming a regular team, called, appropriately enough, since Bolton and Bradley, who made up the team, were also from Lancashire, " The Cloggers."

I was getting to know J. E. S. Jones, referred to earlier in the book as winner of the 1934 Knott Cup Trial. It was the first stages of an acquaintance which was to ripen into a friendship I regarded as a privilege to enjoy. " Jonah " had won one of the precious few, much coveted M.C.C. Triple Awards for a hundred-per-cent success in the 1934 Exeter and the 1935 Land's End and Edinburgh Trials.

After the Motor Cycling Club's Torquay Trial, in the early summer of 1935, I had some conversation with Lewis Welch, leading the " Musketeer " Magnette team. Welch, an Oxford man, had an immense wealth of experience behind him, and had won more M.C.C. Triple Awards than was decent for one man. I was interested to find that the " Musketeer " cars had not been used by Welch, Nash, and Kindell in this event, but, instead, three other ex-racing M.G. cars. These were " P " type Midgets, which had run in the 24-hours Rudge-Whitworth Cup Race at Le Mans, in France. Under the sponsorship of G. E. T. Eyston, famous racing driver and breaker of world's speed records, the cars had been actually driven, turn and turn about, by six girls, the Misses Evans, Skinner, Allan, Richmond, Ellison, and Mrs. Eaton. Since Le Mans the cars had been fitted with the newly introduced 939 c.c., " PB " engines and repainted chocolate and cream.

Also at Torquay was one of the new Triumphs, with the now-almost-universally-adopted flat-backed, external-petrol-tank type of body, first popularized by the old J2 M.G.s. At the wheel was Geoffrey Boughton, from Stratford on Avon, of whom I will say, and I am sure that he would not wish me to say otherwise, that his hobby was Beer !

I met Bira, the well-known racing driver, although I hardly expect him to remember me from so fleeting a meeting. He came to Rushmere on the occasion of the M.G. Car Club staging car events there in the spring of 1935.

The Rushmere " arena " lies just off the main Stourbridge-Bridgnorth road, and was first exploited by the Cygnet Motor and Motor Cycle Club of Bridgnorth for "freak" and "American-type " hill-climbs for motor-cycles. In a switchback field, about a third of a mile square, of which the surface is comprised of short turf and semi-sandy soil, the main obstacle is a wide, straight, but very " sudden " climb with a final pitch of 1 in $1\frac{1}{2}$.

I was standing on the hill before the start, waiting for it to rain, when Bira came up anxiously inquiring where he could buy some competition tyres for the Riley Imp (on a Sunday morning). He had come without such equipment, not altogether realizing the nature of the event.

Technical expert and supercharger specialist M. A. McEvoy was more usually met " behind the scenes," but he drove in a number of events at this period in one of the independently-front-sprung Singer saloons, equipped with a big Zoller supercharger and a solid back axle. Locking the differential mechanism, to produce the effect of a solid back axle, had been found to be a definite aid to obtaining wheelgrip on some of the more freakish types of hill now being used in the trials.

I had had the extreme pleasure, too, of meeting and getting to know Mr. Cecil Kimber, managing director of the M.G. Car Co. Ltd. " Kim," even in business hours, was one of the most " approachable " men I knew. He loved to mix with " the boys," and his tremendous interest in, and regular attendance at, all functions of the M.G. Car Club, social and competitive, was keenly appreciated by those same " boys," and contributed, in very large measure, to the abounding success of the club. I was a little shocked when I heard, after the outbreak of war, that " Kim " had severed his connection with the company that was his own brain-child, but, after a little thought, I felt that, perhaps, I could visualize the background.

There were few events of the M.G. Car Club at which one did not meet George Tuck, publicity manager down at Abingdon, whose charming wife figured so attractively in much of the company's pictorial publicity matter. As might be expected, I knew most of the staff at the works. I first met John Thornley at the time of the upset over my first J2. Thornley, of course, was the man who used to tell you how much it would cost to mend the " bits " you had broken, and a one-time secretary of the M.G. Car Club also. Although, on account of the J2, we rather got off on the wrong foot, business relations blossomed into personal friendship and, while I do not think that John ever really erased his original conception of me as No. 1 pessimist, we had many a good laugh together.

There were few trials drivers who did not, also, like to take some hand in the social side of the various clubs' activities, so that I was delighted to be co-opted on to the committee of the Midland Centre of the M.G. Car Club during 1935. There was a small, but rapidly expanding, core of terrific enthusiasm in the Midland Centre. We turned out in tremendous force, both to compete and to assist, when the main centre of the club came to an arrangement with the Cygnet Motor Cycle Club of Bridgnorth to run car events at Rushmere. When the M.G. Car Club became the M.G. Car Club Limited, instead of staging what secretary Harris called " a dry-as-dust formal inauguration," he

Photo : " The Autocar "

1935 " ABINGDON "—C. W. NASH WITH " ARAMIS " OF THE ORIGINAL " THREE MUSKETEERS "
M.G. MAGNETTE TEAM

Photo : " The Motor "

1935 " LAWRENCE "—C. G. FITT (FORD V8) MAKES THE ONLY
SUCCESSFUL CLIMB OF RED ROADS

put on a " party " at Ivinghoe, and we went along from Birmingham in force, tucked in to a good tea, and afterwards disported ourselves at a grass-tracked hill-climb in some fields on private property close by. We supported the Abingdon Trial in force, too, and to some purpose, Summerfield taking the M.G. Challenge Trophy, Jack Bastock sharing with Michael Lawson (from the Singer Club) the P. J. Evans Trophy, and Crawford, Haden, and myself, as already recorded, taking the inter-centre team award, a performance we had already pulled off in the club's earlier trial in the Chilterns, so that the Midland Centre felt pretty cock-a-hoop.

I remember our staging a very successful gymkhana in a smoother-than-usual field just outside Solihull, finishing up with a relay-race in which competitors shot from one end of the field to the other (and it was a big field), turned abruptly around a post, and returned more or less in their own tracks, so that a good time was had by all, results being announced and prizes awarded over a slap-up tea at " The George " at Solihull.

CHAPTER IV

The "N" Magnette

DURING my ownership of the "P" type, outstanding performances were being achieved by the 1287 c.c., six-cylinder "N" Magnettes, usually in two-seater form, and, ever impetuous, I decided in the early autumn of 1935 that I must have one.

Opinions used to be very divided about the "N" *wagons*. The engine had certain inherent faults peculiar to the "small six" as a type, but it is my considered opinion that the Magnettes were capable of giving more success for less modification (or, if you prefer it, less departure from manufacturer's specification) than any other of the M.G. models with which I had experience. Of those Magnettes which were, at this period (1935 season), consistently successful, I do not think any resorted to putting alternative ratio crown-wheels and pinions in the back-axle, as one did on the J2 Midgets ; and again on the new "PBs" (those that did not sprout a "blower"), nor to stripping off mudguards and pieces of bodywork, as was becoming customary on the "P" type Midgets. It was a good thing to have some stouter axle half-shafts (readily obtainable from the works), and many drivers did have the engine modified more or less to the specification of the cars which ran in the Ulster Tourist Trophy race. This consisted, in the main, of appreciably raising the compression-ratio, fitting very large-bore carburettors and a special distributor with two pairs of points. I had this modification carried out myself, in time, but it is only fair to say that I experienced both successes before and some failures after the modification.

There was a number of much more specialized cars running also. The ex-racing "Musketeer" Magnettes (at this stage un-supercharged) have already been spoken of, and there were three cars running, in the hands of Dennis, Kenneth, and Doreen Evans, which had, not only the modified engines, but altered gear-boxes, giving higher bottom and second gears, and new, narrow, very light bodies, virtually of racing pattern, and the now inevitable J2 Midget-type mudguards.

The Evans family were most prominent in motor sport, both

in trials and in racing, although after about 1935 they tended to concentrate almost entirely on racing and speed events. Miss Evans, in particular, displayed a flair and an aptitude for high-speed work not commonly to be found in members of her sex. Dennis (D. G.) Evans managed the Bellevue Garage on Wandsworth Common, where, in addition to providing the usual facilities required by the ordinary motorist, he maintained a special shop for preparing and tuning racing and competition cars.

When I drove my own Magnette home for the first time, my first impressions, curiously, were not so much of any feature of the performance, though that was quite delightful, but rather of how very much bigger in every way the Magnette felt, very much more so than was actually the case. The first modification I made to my car, after fitting the inevitable plate back and front for holding competition numbers, was to fit in my bucket-seats. I had acquired these during ownership of the " P." Space was at a premium in the driving compartments of the J2 and the " P " type, and I found that the straight-across back-rest tended to impede the movement of the left arm in involved driving tests, or awkward hairpin corners, and also, being rather short, I wanted to sit more on top of the steering wheel and have more support across the shoulders.

When I was down at Abingdon, after the 1934 Gloucester Trial, I found, in the racing department, a pair of well-shaped, firmly made bucket-seats, taken from a J4 racing job, to which the owner had had a special single-seater body fitted. I persuaded the company to let me have these, although they were upholstered in green leather, whereas the " P " type was finished maroon. I took them along to a coach-building and painting firm that I knew well, and asked if they could cellulose them to the required colour. The painters undertook to do the job at my own risk, with no guarantee that the paint would not wear off in use. When I parted with the seats finally, after four years, the original green was showing through faintly, just here and there, where the most rubbing occurred.

Although these seats looked a bit lost in the broader, roomier driving compartment of the Magnette, I plumped for them every time for competition purposes, because of the extra support they gave round the thighs and up the spine, and the added freedom of movement for the left elbow.

At the outset the car was not interfered with mechanically,

and, at the outset, the car failed mechanically. There was a most puzzling and irritating " drying-up " at full throttle, not consistently, but at intervals. At first the trouble defied diagnosis as to whether it was petrol starvation or ignition trouble, and before Lucas's (Joseph Lucas Ltd.) tied it down to the latter, there was failure on Widlake, in the Knott Trophy Trial, and on Bamford Clough, in the M.C.C. " One-Day Sporting." But the Magnette tore up Hatherland, in pouring rain, in a most reassuring manner.

With the Magnette put to rights, I made the long journey down to Riverhill, below Sevenoaks in Kent, to compete in the Singer Club's Bullock Trophy Trial.

The programme went out of its way to apologise for the ease of the course, and W. J. B. Richardson, of the white Singer team, acting on this occasion as secretary of the event, felt justified in barring the use of competition tyres. And then it rained ! Trouble started with the very first of the non-stop hills, Hognore, where a stop-and-go test was scheduled. This rapidly became virtually impossible, and delay among following competitors, of whom there were above seventy, began to assume alarming proportions even here at the very first hill. But it was the next " bank " (Black Country slang for any up-grade, and much used by trials drivers), Whitehorse, that as good as wrecked the event. Whitehorse is a long, narrow hill, on a dry day hardly worth including as a non-stop hill, but that pouring wet Sunday it was a hundred per cent. " stopper."

For me, personally, it was the one bright spot of the trial. Before it was abandoned, both because of the appalling delay as well as the extreme difficulty of the hill, about twenty-five competitors " had a crack " at it, and my Magnette was one of the six cars which did struggle successfully to the top.

It was in the capacity of passenger again that I went, for the second year in succession, on the North-West London Motor Club's Inter-Club Team Trial. I rode with Crawford once again. As in 1934, teams comprised four cars, with the three best performances to count, and Crawford was running as fourth man with the " Musketeer " Magnette trio.

The same course was used as before—" timed climb " round Darracott's three hairpin corners (so called) ; re-start on Mine-shop ; Hackmarsh ; Darracott the reverse way round ; and Cunliffe Lane. Even the weather, by a strange freak of coincidence, reproduced the previous year's conditions, half a gale blowing, little tempered by the wintry sunshine.

I found the by-ways and farm-tracks of North Devon, " far from the madding crowd," most fascinating even in late autumn. From the passenger's seat one has a little more time to study the countryside. What a lovely spot is the foot of Darracott, and I wonder how many people know it, outside of the trials fraternity and the locals ! And also that fascinating run, starting from Bude, which goes right across Widemouth Bay and on, hugging the coast all the way, with one or two really severe gradients (having the inevitable climbing hairpin corners) right to Crackington Haven.

Not all of Crawford's artistry at the wheel, and it was considerable, could get the Magnette away in the Mineshop stop-and-go test, the driving wheels spinning on the greasy shale and rock slab as if on polished ice. With Cunliffe Lane, a non-stop hill, still to be attempted, one of the back tyres went flat. Crawford did not fancy tackling Cunliffe on one competition tyre and one " plain " tyre, which would be the position if we simply brought one of the spares into use. We thought the best thing to do, in consequence, was to take a tube out of one of the tyres then resting on the spare wheels, strip the punctured tube from the competition tyre, and replace with the sound tube. Regrettably we had no tyre levers. Fortunately, my line of business is the maintenance (cum distribution) of pneumatic tyre equipment, and, fortunately again, I had served my time on the practical handling side of the business.

I got to work with a blunt screw-driver and a cylinder-head spanner ! The ordinary tyre did not present much of a problem, the tube was soon stripped out ; but competition tyres used to be of a very stiff build, added to which Crawford had, for some time, been running tyres of 5·25-inch section instead of the standard 4·75-inch section. It was a cold day, but we were stripping off our leather greatcoats long before we were through with the job. The whole performance was carried out with the car jacked up in a narrow lane, between high hedges, with a gradient of about 1 in 5.

There should be a happy ending to this story, but, in the interests of strict accuracy, I have to confess that, although the tyre change was successfully carried through, the Magnette did *not* make a non-stop climb of Cunliffe.

With this event I concluded my second full year of active participation in motor trials, since, in five days' time, on Thursday, October 24th, I would be at my second M.G. Car Club Show-Time Dinner-Dance, again at the Park Lane Hotel.

On the immediately following Saturday there was to be held the rather grandiosely titled " British Experts Invitation Trial," with a start at about 10 a.m. from the little village of Dunster, in North Somerset. Somewhat to my surprise I had found, after a careful check of my records, that I was just about eligible for this event (eligibility being the requirement to have won either nine first-class awards, or six first- and six second-class awards, in certain " recognized " events). I planned to go to Park Lane on the Thursday evening, the Motor Show on Friday morning, travel across to the west country after lunch, and compete in the trial on the Saturday. The problem of where to spend the Friday night was delightfully solved when J. E. S. Jones and his wife kindly asked me to spend it at their home at Bruton, which lies a little south-east of Shepton Mallet.

There were all the makings of a cheery three days, but there was one factor I had reckoned without. On the Thursday morning, as I was preparing to set out for London, I fell ill with stomach disorders. I was loath to give up the projected outing, and I decided, rather rashly, to try a bit of that " mind-over-matter " business. At first " matter " tended to get the upper hand. I had an uncomfortable ride down from Birmingham, and although I struggled to the dinner-dance, I had to leave again, even before the dinner part of the function was over. I had a wretched night, but the next morning (Friday) the thing seemed to be wearing itself out a bit, and I went along to the Motor Show, where I was fortified on port and brandies by supercharger expert Michael McEvoy.

The journey out from London, across to Bruton, was only slightly interrupted. I picked up with Mrs. A. E. Moss in her familiar white, $1\frac{1}{2}$-litre Singer *en route*, and we ran for a long way in company. I spent a quiet evening with " Jonah " and his wife, and after a much better night's sleep, I set out for the trial on the Saturday morning more hopefully.

From its inception, in the autumn of 1933, the " Experts " had been an avowedly hell-for-leather, tough, he-man's trial, but the regulations for the 1935 event banned competition tyres and also locked-differentials—for an event on Exmoor, at the end of October ! It looked, for a time, as though the organizing club might not get its entry, and fierce controversy raged. But the organizers, the Mid-Surrey Automobile Club, stuck to their guns, and the trial went through. When a wet and slippery Widlake was actually climbed, by one of the new 2-litre sports Frazer-Nash-B.M.W.s, driven by H. G. Symmons, criticism of the organizers' methods was rather knocked on the head.

I felt better during the trial than at any other time during the week-end, " mind " getting the upper hand at last. Although Widlake proved to be beyond the Magnette's capabilities, the car gave an exemplary performance otherwise, and collected an award for " best performance in the 1500 c.c. Class." Thereafter " matter " beat " mind " completely, and I was ill for several days afterwards.

Crawford has occasion to remember the 1935 Experts Trial. He had experienced difficulty in securing the services of a passenger, and actually arrived at the start without one. This problem was solved when he. was able to enlist the help of A. B. Langley, who had turned up in the rôle of spectator, on the basis, presumably, of " the onlooker sees most of the game." Langley quickly resumed the rôle of spectator ! At the first hill the gear-box disintegrated on Crawford's car. He was, actually, left with top and reverse gears still operative, and in this condition the car was driven (!) all the way back to Wolverhampton.

Being a glutton for punishment, I arranged to compete in two trials in the space of one week-end. On the Saturday there was the Bristol Motor Cycle and Light Car Club's first Roy Fedden Trophy Trial, and, on the Sunday, the Sunbeam Motor Cycle Club's Car Trial, starting between Farnborough and Aldershot.

Both events went off well, although there was a failure at Bristol, the Magnette spinning to a standstill just above the sharp corner on Uplands, a one-time motor-cycle hill, and quite a " proposition." Indeed, only two cars managed to climb non-stop, so that my Magnette's successful negotiation of the rest of the course was still good enough to bring in the award for " the best performance over 1100 c.c."

I saw J. E. S. Jones experience one of those unfortunate mishaps which befall most of us at times. The hill was deceptive on the lower reaches, and "Jonah's " " PB " Midget suddenly and most unexpectedly slid into a ditch on the right-hand side, nearly capsizing. The car was man-handled out, Jones took off a second time—and made a perfect non-stop climb. Unfortunately the slide into the ditch had occurred after the car had passed the " Observed Section Begins " notice, so that failure had been already recorded.

As officials of the organizing clubs were always posted on the non-stop hills to observe and record competitors' performances thereon, " Observed " was equally as suitable a description as " Non-stop " for these sections, and the two terms were synonymous in the trials vocabulary.

Waiting for my run in the special test, I got talking to another driver whom I found had come down from Birmingham for the trial, C. D. Buckley. Buckley was just starting in trials, driving a white sports Austin Seven. He was tremendously enthusiastic, and, right from the start, showed an unusual flair for involved " against-the-clock " tests.

At the start on the Sunday morning, it was gradually borne in upon me, as I looked round the assembled cars, that the bulk of the entry was comprised of the " heavy brigade," mostly Ford V8's. They were not, however, the fairly sedate, streamlined saloons and coupés one was accustomed to meet in events like the " Land's End," and whose comfortable interiors I had secretly envied during the night sections of the long-distance trials, but low, fierce, open-bodied monsters, with sketchy mudguards and lots of spare wheels, shod with huge section tyres having a sort of swastika-pattern tread of great depth. Guy Warburton's well-tried, " 30/98 " Vauxhall was there, too, to augment the heavy brigade.

This trial, at its inception, was to have been of the " Lawrence Cup " type, with sections on War Department territory around Frensham, but, unfortunately, at the eleventh hour there was a sudden descent of large numbers of Territorials on to the area to have been used, and the organizers had hastily to devise a new course in the Surrey hills ! The trial seemed to me, though why I cannot tell you, to be one of the longest events, outside of the M.C.C. " classics," in which I had driven. Such was not, in fact, the case, and probably I was tired.

Whiling away a little time outside a time-check I talked at some length with C. M. Anthony. I hoped I might find out how he got his 1½-litre, T.T. replica Aston Martin round trials courses on a supposedly " impossibly " high gear of around 14 : 1.

The Magnette went great guns, climbing all the non-stop

hills, but could not match the terrific initial acceleration of the V8 Fords in the timed-climb test, which selected, from among the handful of us who came through without fault, the outright winner. This proved to be one of the " low, fierce, open-bodied monsters," driven by S. H. Allard, from London, at this stage a driver unknown to me.

The next week-end I was able to play on my own " muck-heap," when Sunbac ran the Shell Cup Trial in Worcestershire. First surprise came, not from finding the course to be of any particular severity, it was all-familiar ground, but from finding the three " Musketeer " Magnettes, hitherto handled mainly by Welch, Kindell, and Nash, now being driven by R. A. Macdermid and J. A. Bastock, of the " Cream Cracker " Midget team, and A. B. Langley from the white Singer team.

Bastock's " Cracker " Midget appeared in the hands of A. H. Langley, customarily seen in the 1½-litre Singer, and M. G. Billingham drove brother Langley's white Singer, in fact, quite a " general post."

Maurice Toulmin turned up with a sort of fixed coupé top on his " Cream Cracker " Midget, which gave rise to a deal of good-natured leg-pulling and rude remarks about hen-coops and things.

It was from Toulmin I learned that the " Musketeer " Magnettes would continue to be driven by Macdermid, Bastock, and Langley (A. B.), by arrangement with the M.G. factory, while Toulmin himself was to form a new " Cream Cracker " team, it being whispered that three new and rather special cars were to be provided. Later, Crawford told me that he was almost certain to join Toulmin in the formation of the new team, and that the most likely candidate for third place was J. E. S. Jones. He could give me no particular clue as to the likely make-up of the new cars, except that, basically, they would be the 9 h.p., 939 c.c. " PB " Midgets.

In the December issue of " Mit " Harris's monthly magazine *The Sports Car* was a photograph bearing the following caption : " Here's a lovely village—Hartland in North Devon on the south side of Barnstaple Bay. The little square is filled by a few of the cars which competed in the North-West London Motor Club's Inter-Club Team Trial. Many competitors in trials owe much of their keenness for the sport to the beautiful places to which their hobby takes them."

In my case, at any rate, the last paragraph was very true. Two years of driving in motor trials had taken me the length and breadth of my country, barring the flat east coast, and given me the most comprehensive geography lesson obtainable. In those years just before the present war, surely no section of the community, not even the commercial traveller, saw so much of its own countryside and of the beautiful parts in particular, as the regular trials driver. The Cotswolds, the Chilterns, the hills of Wales, the Derbyshire dales, Exmoor, North Devon, the coasts of Cornwall, parts of Kent, Surrey (particularly around Hindhead and Petersfield), the Lake District, parts of the Mendips, the Clee Hills, parts of Worcestershire, were all " trials country."

In my own case again, trials had aroused in me an all-absorbing enthusiasm which the field sports such as golf, tennis, etc., had never awakened. Apart from the expense which was inevitable if a big programme was undertaken, I revelled in every aspect of the trials game and applied myself assiduously to it. So immense was my enthusiasm that at times it tended to get out of hand, and an occasional set-back was liable to be taken too seriously, with unnecessary heart burning, so that one had to pull oneself up with a jerk, lest one's mood be misconstrued as that of a bad loser. Over-enthusiasm, temporarily rebuffed by the slings and arrows of misfortune, can easily create such an impression, but such a mood is, to my way of thinking, very different to that of the man who has come into a game merely to win and is upset because someone else has beaten him to it. I suffered, too, from over-anxiety, arising out of a grim determination not to allow myself to be written off in trials as the failure that I had been in the field sports, so that there were, I know well, occasions, after I had given a particularly puerile exhibition of driving, when the old brow was unduly furrowed and temporary moods of depression descended.

To resume, on November 22nd, the Midland Centre of the M.G. Car Club, held its own dinner-dance at the New Billesley Arms, King's Heath, success being assured when we persuaded Mr. Kimber to come up from Abingdon and take the chair, strongly supported by F. L. M. Harris, a tower of strength at any party.

Talking of parties, did you ever go to one of the club's " downstage " affairs ? If you did, you will scarcely want reminding of these mad and glorious affairs, but in case you didn't, let me tell you about the one I went to at the King's Arms at Berkhamp-stead, on December 14th. First, to give you the general mood, let me quote you some words of Harris's from the pages of *The Sports Car* : ". . . it should not be a ' five-star ' hotel, but one of the kind at which early arrivals could play a game of darts in the taproom (the taproom being the only place where the dart-board would be found at this date). It would be well if the proprietor were accustomed to a few odds and ends getting broken towards the end of the evening."

The key for the whole evening's proceedings was set by the engaging of a band of genuine street musicians, not a regular professional orchestra dressed for the part, but honest-to-goodness theatre-queue " buskers." They were equipped exclusively with brass instruments and made absolutely no concession whatsoever to the fact that, for the first time, they were playing under a roof. The row was terrific, and their performance was almost non-stop. First " interruption " was provided by Mrs. Harris, who rushed in, dressed as a Salvation Army Lass, and presented Mr. Kimber with a huge " chain of office " hung with medallions reading " President, Captain, Starter, Judge, Trustee, and Gent." Shortly afterwards a member alleged not to have paid his sub-scription was led in in convict's garb, manacled to a " spoof " policewoman, again the ubiquitous Mrs. Harris, the convict, if I remember rightly, being Robin Mere. Harris himself was formally presented with a white helmet, and one or two people got up and made speeches, but as no one had thought to tell the band to stop playing while they did so, and somebody also let off a collection of fireworks, not all of them of the indoor type, nobody knows what was said. Weird and peculiar things happened to the cutlery. The party quietened temporarily after the meal had been cleared away, and was entertained by the popular music-hall artist Freddie Bamberger, who fitted his patter to the occasion with enormous success. In a final burst of revelry Macdermid put in a terrific rugby tackle, only to find that board floors are less yielding than grass fields, to the detriment of his collar-bone. Oh, it was quite a party : a different venue had to be found for the following year's event.

When the regulations appeared for the 1935 London–Gloucester Trial, run the first week-end in December, the organizers, the North-West London Motor Club, reserved to themselves the right to include, if deemed advisable on the day, an additional hill not shown on the printed route-card. Many drivers concluded that this would be the very difficult Juniper hill, rising straight off the " old " Painswick-Stroud road, so that when a little knot of officials arrived there for a look round, at the week-end preceding the trial, they found quite a few drivers " trying out " the hill. Among them were Geoffrey Boughton with his Triumph, and Crawford and myself on our Magnettes. Crawford had theories about concentrating weight directly over the back axle to check wheelspin, and had come along with a number of heavy iron floor-gratings in the back of the M.G. There seemed to be something in it, and I had a couple of two-gallon petrol tins filled with lead shot, and arranged them on a little platform contrived on the chassis cross-member just behind the axle.

Probably you remember that the 1935 " Gloucester " was the one in which, at the start from " The Spider's Web," on the Watford by-pass, a policeman guided competitors through almost impenetrable fog to the opposite side of the broad by-pass, and having shown them the kerb, sent them hopefully (!) on their way. What an awful night ! I was early in trouble. I found myself off route in the first mile or two, and at one point was actually heading back into London. One wondered if it was all worth while. On the preceding Tuesday I had gone to bed with a severe chill and had been forced to do another of those " mind-over-matter " stunts to get to the start. It was not until the Thursday morning that I got fixed up with a passenger, Vivian Woodward, one of Bastock's regular passengers, coming to my aid, Bastock having made other arrangements on this occasion.

We plodded on, but, so thick was the fog that it was impossible to pick up any of the usual landmarks, and for miles I was in a sweat of uncertainty whether we had, or had not, got back on to the proper route. Then, of a sudden there shot past me the " Candidi Provocatores " Singer Nine team, doing a good 30 m.p.h. at least. (Avery having retired from active trials participation, and Langley gone over to the " Musketeer " M.G. team, W. J. B. Richardson had formed a new trio with M. H. Lawson and A. C. Westwood. The team name was interpreted to mean " the White Challengers," the three new type Le Mans Singer Nines, which the team drove, being painted a gleaming white.) I had heard before that Lawson, who was leading, had cat's eyes and could see in the dark. The rumour appeared to have been founded on fact.

I tucked in behind them, focusing my eyesight on the ruby gleam that was the third car's rear-light. But, after a very few miles, I simply had to fall back. I rarely remember anything so hectic. I did not know whether I was on the right or the wrong side of the road, or even if I was on the road at all. I do not mean to imply by this that the Singer boys were a public danger, or that they were driving with a callous disregard for the safety of any other road users who might be out on such a night. There are people who can get along in fog, and also in darkness, where many another person is absolutely stranded, and there is no doubt that Lawson was particularly gifted in this direction.

Suddenly, just like drawing a curtain aside, the fog lifted almost completely. I had not dared to look at a watch to know just how much time had been lost crawling about in the fog. Although the time schedule for the night section had required an average of only around 20 m.p.h., it was obvious that nothing approaching that speed had, in fact, been maintained, so that, as the fog lifted, I opened flat out to try to get back on schedule. A wicked slide on the first corner, and a peculiar " lightness " about the steering, then made me realize that the roads were icebound, a fact which had not shown up at the very slow speeds at which we had been crawling about in the fog.

The subsequent mad " dice " (from the expression so often used by the daily press when referring to motor sport, " diceing with death ") to try to make the time check at Chipping Camden on time was an experience long to be remembered. The Magnette came down the hill, and drew into the check, just two minutes late ! Subsequently, in view of the exceptional weather conditions, the organizers decided, in the compiling of the results, to exact no penalty for late arrival at any of the time checks *en route*.

From this point onwards, it was a severe, eminently sporting, and altogether enjoyable trial. After a more than usually welcome breakfast in the wee, sma' hours, at " The Plough," at Cheltenham, we set out to climb Bismore, Mutton, Quarhouse, Ham Mill, Old Hollow, Juniper (yes ! Juniper was included), Mill Lane, and Nailsworth Ladder. The Magnette was bang on form again, but, even so, I was genuinely though very pleasantly surprised when it romped up Juniper non-stop.

My heart bled for my team-mate, Bill Haden. Haden was the only competitor in the running for a Gloucester Goblet, which is given for a clean sheet three years in succession. This was also Haden's last trial, so that he had set his heart on winning a Goblet. But Juniper proved just a bit too severe for the game " P " type : it seemed a cruel stroke of fate.

I was in company, during a good portion of the day section, with the " Musketeer " Magnettes, and I learned that Macdermid's car was running supercharged, and was giving a simply terrific performance. I was told afterwards that his climb of Nailsworth Ladder was one of the most spectacular things seen there in years, the Magnette leaping high in the air, with all four wheels well clear of the ground, over the famous bumps.

I think it can be truthfully said that it was the " Gloucester " that finally put S. H. Allard " in the headlines." With the " low, fierce, open-bodied monster," which I had first met some weeks previously in the Sunbeam Club's trial—actually one of the special Ford V8's which competed in the 1934 Ulster Tourist Trophy Race—Allard nearly, though not quite, equalled Macdermid's startling times in the three timed-climb tests which were held, and was outstanding on all the observed hills, particularly at Juniper. He ran Macdermid very close indeed for the Gloucester Cup, and was rewarded with the North-West London Cup for " best performance in the unlimited class."

Our old friend Onslow Bartlett enlivened the " Gloucester." Instead of the familiar green Magnette, he was driving a much-battered and, at any rate in appearance, entirely decrepit, old " M " type Midget, entirely innocent of windscreen and with the bodywork (!) cut to an irreducible minimum and mudguards (so called) of the sketchiest. But the engine, it was said, had been " attended to " by McEvoy's (the tuning wizards at Derby), and certainly it must be told that he very, very nearly climbed Juniper.

At " The Bear," on Rodborough Common, after the finish I met Dennis Buckley again, and was delighted to hear that he had brought the little Austin through without fault. I had a word also with Alf Langley. He had been driving the ex-Bastock " Cream Cracker " Midget again, instead of the more usual 1½-litre Singer. Langley secured the President's Trophy for " best performance up to 850 c.c."

The " London–Exeter " date was brought forward, so that

the start came the night after Boxing Night. I had entered, but, eventually, I was a non-starter. It came about this way. I spent the Christmas period away from home at the newly opened Norbury House Hotel at Droitwich Spa. My original plan was to leave Droitwich after lunch on Boxing Day, run back to my home on the outskirts of Birmingham to change into suitable clothing for the trial, then pick up my passenger, who lived near by, and drive down to London for the start of the event. A sudden unsteadiness about the back of the car during the short run over from Droitwich to my home suggested shock-absorber trouble. Hasty investigation showed my fears to be well founded, and, moreover, that the trouble was such that I had not the facilities to correct it. There might be the labour available to handle the repair down at Lucas's (of whose manufacture the shock-absorber was)—such a firm often maintaining a skeleton emergency staff even on a public holiday—but time was the dominant factor.

I was not keen to take the car through the trial as it stood. It might have got through, but I felt that it would have been a wearing ride, haunted throughout by the expectation of still further breakage, and I was already tired from the Christmas festivities. I rang up my passenger, Douglas Barwell. Barwell was a pillar of strength of the Sunbac Club, a competent wielder of the stop-watch, and a marshal and observer of long experience. He had made every possible preparation for the trip, and was bitterly disappointed when I suggested calling it off. He appreciated that time scarcely permitted of a repair being carried through before we set off to the start, but he tried everything to persuade me to make a sporting attempt to get the car through as it was. I do not think that he ever forgave me for finally deciding not to make the trip.

As a result, I was not present at the début of the new " Cream Cracker " M.G. Midget team, of which the personnel, as surmised, comprised Toulmin, Crawford, and Jones. It was a happy début, the three new cars tying with the now firmly established " Musketeer " Magnette trio—all three cars of this team now supercharged—for the " Exeter " team prize.

Because these new " Cream Cracker " M.G.s were " works " cars—that is, they were directly sponsored by the factory and maintained by M.G. for one specific purpose, to obtain success in trials—there was a tendency in many quarters to think of them as super-special cars, having but little in common with the more standard " PB " models off the normal production line. In point of fact they were not super-special. I know, because I was enabled to purchase one of these three cars later on.

The engines were fitted with superchargers, but even this device for boosting power was nothing unusual on trials cars, as described in the chapter " Uphill Work." Probably the works cars " blew " at slightly higher pressures, but no basic alterations were carried out to the engine on that account. The gear-box and clutch were quite standard, as, also, was the final drive and differential assembly at the outset. Later, however, new crown wheels and pinions, having straight-cut teeth, were employed, and stouter axle-shafts, to withstand the tremendous twisting stresses. Frequently the cars ran with the differential mechanism locked, to produce a " solid " axle effect.

The cars certainly differed from standard in having the bodies panelled in aluminium, with bonnets of the same material, though the use of the light J2-type mudguards as a still further weight-saving measure was not uncommon on competition cars. The shock-absorbing arrangements were non-standard, a pair of Hartford telecontrol type being fitted at the rear, controlled instantly by a big handle under the instrument panel. The front suspension was steadied by two pairs of shock-absorbers, one friction, one hydraulic.

Two spare wheels were carried, of course, and the rear number-plate and lamp were moved to a less vulnerable position high up on the offside mudguard. Two petrol pumps were fitted, separately controlled. The blower was driven by twin belts off a special pulley fitted to the nose of the crankshaft, and lubricated from a dash-pot of exactly the same type as used for automatic centralized chassis lubrication on cars like the Rover.

The mudguards, front tray, and top panels of the bonnets were painted chocolate, the remainder of the car cream, with the wheels finished in aluminium. Toulmin drove JB 7521, Crawford JB 7524, and Jones JB 7525.

Photo : "The Autocar"

1935 " GLOUCESTER "—H. K. CRAWFORD (M.G. MAGNETTE) LEAPS GAILY
UP NAILSWORTH LADDER

Photo : "The Autocar"

1936 "CREAM CRACKER" M.G. TEAM

Left to right : J. E. S. JONES, H. K. CRAWFORD, J. M. TOULMIN. WITH TOULMIN IS LEWIS WELCH

CHAPTER V

1936

EARLY in the new year—1936—I called, in the normal way of business, on Norman Terry. Terry, of course, is a directo1 of Herbert Terry Ltd., the kings of spring (if I may coin a phrase). I found that he had purchased one of the 2-litre, two-seater, sports Frazer-Nash-B.M.W.s, and was planning a big trials programme. He took me a run round, it seemed pretty " useful." About the same time I learned that Dennis Buckley was going to have a new Austin Seven, with a Centric super-charger on the engine, and bodywork of the now so generally adopted J2 pattern. The three of us decided to band together to go after the team award in the forthcoming Colmore Trophy Trial.

Meantime I went down, with a big party from the Midland Centre of the M.G. Car Club, for the main centre's Chilterns Trial, starting from Marlow. On arrival at Marlow I found that the rear shock-absorber had collapsed again. As the start was not until 11 a.m. the next morning, there seemed a sporting chance of effecting repairs if I got on the job with the local garage bright and early. But we ran into unforeseen problems, and, at the time at which I should have gone to the starting line, the wretched thing was still in pieces. Eventually some sort of order was restored, and I went along to see how competitors were faring on Crowell. There was thick snow everywhere, which had frozen hard overnight ; the non-stop hills were prov-ing very difficult. The ground falls away badly on the right-hand side of Crowell, about three parts of the way up. I had always eyed it warily and thought that it had possibilities, and that afternoon I actually saw a competing car overturn there and slide away down the bank. The driver was thrown clear, but the passenger suffered head injuries and was taken to hospital. Happily they did not prove serious. Thereafter I went to Abing-don and got the shock-absorber problem really straightened out.

1936 " Colmore "—remember how it rained ! As I filled up with petrol at Broadway, *en route* to the start, the sky was almost jet black, and it was already spotting. Sunbac had got a new hill : it was a little, beaten-earth track up through trees, on the upper slopes of Fish Hill, above Broadway, actually another hill from the route of the motor-cycle " Colmore."

Unfortunately there was no proper approach to the hill. After leaving the main road, by a gate on the left, as you descended Fish Hill back towards Broadway, you went along a narrow track among the ferns and little new trees, and then, suddenly, had to descend a quite steep grassy bank and turn round in a muddy field, to come up to the foot of the hill proper. As the threatening skies made good their threat, and the rain fell in torrents, the negotiation of the grassy bank became tricky, to say the least of it, while the turning round in the field became well-nigh impossible without assistance, so that the massive horses, which Sunbac wisely had standing by, were used, not so much for getting away competing cars which failed on the hill itself—the surface of the hill itself deteriorated very little—but rather for hauling cars out of the field and getting them to the foot of the hill. Many competitors, brought to the line behind the horses, managed to get away and make a non-stop climb of the hill itself. Such was my own experience. The Magnette slid sideways down the grassy bank, floundered in the field, was hooked up behind a whacking great horse and yanked through the mud to the " Observed Section Begins " notice, and then got away from the line like a perfect little gentleman and climbed non-stop.

In such circumstances cumulative delay was inevitable and, as the rain continued to fall relentlessly, conditions for competitors waiting to make their attempt became pretty grim. It was with the utmost reluctance that marshal-in-charge Bill Vincent (always entrusted with Sunbac's more " sticky " assignments) called it off, after as many as seventy cars had been got on to the hill.

At the foot of Kineton I found Bill Haden, looking, and I think feeling, like a drowned rat, the peak of his soaking cap jammed down over his eyes and his sodden leather coat buttoned up to his chin. I was in little better state myself. I was without a hat, and my hair was wringing wet, and water from it was running down my neck and right down my back and all down my face (somehow one never thought of erecting the hood ; anyhow it wasn't " done " on trials). I had a scarf wound round my neck and the old leather coat buttoned up to the chin, but I could feel water trickling down my chest, very cold water, and pools kept forming on my lap.

The Magnette climbed Kineton, in fact it climbed everything that day, and went like a scalded cat, but it must be confessed that the greatest measure of satisfaction obtained that day was derived, not from the Magnette's excellent performance, but from the hot baths in which we luxuriated at " The Plough," at Cheltenham, where we had booked rooms for the night, while our clothes dried out before the gas-fires in the bedrooms. The passenger was the lady later to become my fiancée, and then my wife, but since at this stage we were not engaged, I was not able to inquire too deeply as to which layer of garments the rain had penetrated to in her case, but I must say she never asked for the hood to be put up.

That same evening Sunbac threw a party at " The Plough," and after dinner provisional results of the trial were announced. They made good listening : Terry, Buckley, and myself had gained the team award, and each of us had, respectively, made best performance of the day in his particular horse-power class.

On the morrow there was to be a match trial between Sunbac and the North-West London Motor Club. The procedure was that there would be eight drivers on each side, each driver to have a private match against his respective opposite number, and the sum of the matches won by each club to decide the result, rather on the lines of golf practice. Those of us who were to compete in this match trial were now told who were to be our opposite numbers, and I learned that I was paired with Guy Warburton.

In the morning the Magnette refused to start. Investigation revealed water in both carburettor float-chambers, and the carburettor pistons also stuck with wet and spots of rust already beginning to form. Yes, it certainly rained that day.

Proceedings opened with a timed climb up Stancombe, and once again I let the over-anxiety bug get me. Determined to justify Sunbac's esteem in picking me to take part in this match, I overdid it and flashed into the first corner far too fast. For a moment I thought that I was not going to get round at all ; the Magnette struck the bank with its near-side front wheel, so that later I found every spoke broken, came back on to the course, and went on, without actually having come to a complete stand-still, but the time was ruined. I went from bad to worse when

the Magnette sunk, almost literally, in the quagmire that was
Cold Slad Hill, while Warburton ploughed through with a bow-
wave like a battleship in a heavy sea. I had hopes of recovering
a " hole " at Juniper, but, just when I thought I had got away
with it, the Magnette spun hectically to a standstill almost in a
split second. Breathlessly I watched Warburton come tearing
up through the trees, slewing from side to side. The old Vauxhall slid to a standstill, wheels furiously churning, exactly on the
same spot as had the Magnette, a " half " ! We halved the rest
of the course, too, Nailsworth Ladder and Ham Mill, so that
Warburton won our match, but Sunbac won the event ; Toulmin,
Laird, Terry, Jones, Crawford, and Alf Langley beating Allard,
Symmons, D. H. Murray, Miss Joan Richmond, G. J. Rea, and
Ben Richardson, while Billingham and Anthony drew their
match.

There was another of these match trials, shortly afterwards,
when the Lancs and Cheshire Club accepted Sunbac's challenge,
but asked us to go and fight it out on their " muck-heap," which
involved the long journey up to Kendal, most of the selected
route lying around the Lakes. We went up on a Saturday
afternoon and evening, played out the match on the Sunday—
it should have been Sunday morning, but, as so often happens
with a difficult course, the thing stretched out until nearly dark,
and then we had the long run home to Birmingham, so that, for
me at any rate, it made rather a tiring week-end. I was again
drawn against one of the " heavy " brigade, T. C. Wise, with
another of the now-much-in-evidence, open-bodied V8 Fords.
The north-country lads certainly showed us some rare lines in
hills. There was a fierce thing called Sadgill, which few of us
managed to climb, and another, of which I cannot now recall
the name, on which I do not think any competitor actually
reached the top and on which I twisted one of the Magnette's
wheels to a horrible shape. Sunbac won the day again, but it
was a close contest and a severe one. This time I just managed
to keep my end up.

A word about organization. Any club affiliated to the Royal
Automobile Club could apply to the parent body, once in each
twelve months, for a permit to run an " open-by-invitation "
trial. To this could be invited the members of five other affiliated
clubs. All other events organized during the same twelve months
period would be open only to the club's own members.

The North-West London Motor Club generally made the "Gloucester" their open-by-invitation trial, but the old-established Coventry Cup Trial was chosen instead, for 1936, and the nature of this usually rather mild event radically altered by the selection of a course in the Exmoor district, with a start, on a Saturday morning, just outside Bridgwater.

I went down to Bridgwater on the Friday evening, the Magnette seeming in fine fettle. Things were buzzing at the "Royal Clarence." Warburton was there with the old "30/98"; Buckley also, with the supercharged Austin. There were some more of the new type, "blown" Sevens there, besides Buckley's, and I met his team-mates, both Birmingham men, H. L. Hadley and W. H. Scriven. Hadley, of course, went on to do big things in the racing world with the twin-O.H.C., single-seater Austins, and Scriven you will probably remember from his shattering imitations of Pop-eye! The Austin boys evolved the team name of "The Grasshoppers."

At the start, the next morning S. H. Allard came up behind me. Although, as recently as the preceding September, Allard had actually been eligible for, and incidentally had won, the Novice Award in a trial (West Hants Club's Knott Trial), he was now very much a force to be reckoned with. Things had been done to the ex-T.T. Ford. The chassis had been shortened, the "low, fierce, open body" had been scrapped entirely and replaced with one from a Grand Prix Bugatti, the Bugatti bonnet also being used and proving a few inches too short, so that the first bit of the engine, just behind the radiator, was uncovered. So far as I can remember, the radiator was not altered at this stage, and I think the car was without windscreen or any form of weather protection. Thus was born the original Allard Special.

In the M.G. teams, for this event, Crawford and Bastock had changed cars, Crawford having a first taste of a "Musketeer." Toulmin's "Cream Cracker" Midget was being driven by Lewis Welch, Toulmin not having found it convenient to make the long journey down from his home near Preston, in Lancashire. Welch proved a worthy substitute for the indomitable Toulmin, and in a severe but thoroughly sporting event, returned the only clean sheet. This did not, however, win for him the Coventry Cup itself, since this, by the conditions attaching to its original presentation to the club for competition, was available only to members, so that Welch took the Exford Cup (best visitor).

Proceedings opened with a new hill, but only two failures were recorded, and the hill was chiefly worth while for the beautiful scenery in which it was set. For that matter, the whole course lay through lovely surroundings. Next came the first special test, accelerating downhill to cross a line, stopping, and reversing back up the hill over the original starting-line. The terrific power of the bored-out, supercharged engines of the " Musketeer " Magnettes was severely straining the transmission on these cars, and this test proved too much for Macdermid's car, the crown-wheel stripping in no uncertain manner. All the M.G. boys carried spare, complete differential units, and Macdermid and his passenger effected a change in less than half an hour : pretty good going !

Widlake was well up to form, and failures were the order of the day, but I saw Crawford make a terrific climb with Bastock's Magnette, and, as he had already made fastest time on the special test, it looked as though he would not be sorry that he had changed cars for the day. For a few glorious seconds I thought that I was going to get away with it myself on Widlake. The Magnette actually got to within sight of the " Observed Section Ends " notice before it finally spun helplessly to a standstill. Incidentally, reversing down Widlake, from as high up as this, is quite a performance, and very hard on the neck muscles.

A little way up the main road off which Widlake runs, but leading off the opposite side of the road, is a hill, not often used, called West Howetown, and here I very nearly " bought it." About half-way up, the hill doubles back on itself, in an acute left-hand hairpin, with a greasy surface on the corner and mud above. There was a timed climb round the hairpin. The Magnette went into a wild front-wheel slide on the apex of the hairpin, but exhorted by W. J. Brunell (the professional photographer who attended most trials), who duly photographed the incident, I recovered and got away. The Kershams were quite " mild " after Widlake, and after lunch at the delightful old " Luttrell Arms," in Dunster, the route led to familiar Doverhay, outside Porlock.

Yet another timed climb was taken here, including both corners. Macdermid promptly stripped another crown-wheel, but, in no wise dismayed, immediately set to work to effect another change, borrowing Arch Langley's spare unit for the purpose, and completed the job in even less time than was taken for the first change. He had climbed Widlake after the first breakage, and went on to climb Cloutsham after this second breakage ! Fastest at Doverhay was Crawford again, but, alas, the " Musketeer " came adrift at the final hurdle, and spun to a standstill on Cloutsham.

Cloutsham was new to me, although I knew it well by repute, and it looked pretty grim : failures were again the order of the day. I remembered a " how to climb Cloutsham and be happy " chat I had had with Arch Langley, who had climbed it to win the 1934 Experts Trial—" take both corners as wide as possible, throttle steady, *particularly* after the first corner." But could I put it all into practice in the heat of the moment ? Yes, I could, and did, and won the Coventry Cup.

I have described this event in some detail, as it was a very good trial, and I would like to take one more paragraph and give you, in this instance, the full results :

Exford Cup (best visitor).—L. A. Welch (M.G. Midget S.).

Brendon Cup (best visitor, opposite class).—H. K. Crawford (M.G. Magnette S.)..

Coventry Cup (best N.W.L.).—C. A. N. May (M.G. Magnette) ; Runner-up, N. V. Terry (Frazer-Nash-B.M.W.).

Whittingham Trophy (best N.W.L. opposite class).—R. Sanford (Fiat) ; Runner-up, S. Curry (M.G. Midget).

Best Sunbac.—H. L. Hadley (Austin S.).

Best M.G. Car Club.—J. E. S. Jones (M.G. Midget S.).

Best J.C.C.—Miss K. Taylor (M.G. Midget).

Gwynne Cup (Team Award).—Crawford, Welch, Jones.

Special Complimentary Awards.—R. A. Macdermid (M.G. Magnette S.) ; W. L. Jackson (Frazer-Nash) ; G. T. I. Taylor (Singer) ; F. Allot (Ford V8) ; A. B. Langley (M.G. Magnette S.).

Third-Class Awards.—A. C. Westwood (Fiat) ; G. T. I. Taylor (Singer) ; S. Peachey (Frazer-Nash-B.M.W.) ; J. A. Bastock (M.G. Magnette S.) ; S. L. Chappell (Ford V8) ; W. S. Whittard (M.G. Midget) ; Mrs. A. E. Moss (Marendaz) ; C. D. Buckley (Austin S.) ; W. J. B. Richardson, A. G. Imhof (Singers).

With the " Coventry " the Magnette reached its peak, and it is a bit hard, thereafter, to have to record that the rest of its trials history, at any rate while it remained in my hands, is a story of failure.

Some week or two after the " Coventry " I was persuaded, very much against my better judgment, to take part in a club race meeting on the short, inner circuit at Donington Park. I have always thought that it was to the " towling " I gave it there that could be traced most of the subsequent troubles.

The fact remains, anyway, that in the Land's End Trial, following soon after, the clutch began to slip even before the breakfast stop was reached. As if that was not in itself sufficient to worry about, one of the flexible petrol pipes sprung a bad leak. With time in hand before the breakfast check, on the outskirts of Taunton, I set about trying to put the house in order. Toulmin tried to come to my rescue ; he had a sound piece of piping but with damaged unions, so we tried to get the unions off my leaky piping and make one good length out of the two. The minutes slipped by and we were making no headway. Toulmin had to go on into the check or he would have been late. My time was coming up and I was getting in a worse state than ever. I shoved one of the lengths of piping back on the car and fled into Taunton with petrol pouring out. Although it was early there was a garage open, but they could not help me. But at breakfast someone came to my rescue with a spare length of pipe with the correct unions at the ends, but when this, in its turn, sprang a leak within only a few miles of restarting after breakfast, I nearly wept. Finally, lengths of adhesive tape were secured, and the leak almost, though not entirely, cured, but the clutch still slipped.

So we went on, and somehow I coaxed it up hill after hill without failure, Station, the Roost, even the re-start at Barton Steep, though I doubt if I was within bogey time ; Darracott too, so that I was beginning to breathe more freely when we came to Bude, for the lunch stop, and things had got no worse. But the first test that would have to be faced after lunch was an " up-down-up " test on Crackington (my old friend Mineshop) : two re-starts together, and all against-the-clock, it looked very much as if this might prove to be the Magnette's Waterloo. If, on the other hand, I did get away with it at Crackington, I felt that the Magnette would then go through to the finish. Well, I did manage Crackington, but I did not reach Land's End. The finish came at Hustyn. There was one loud ominous crack, the engine "raced," and the car "failed to maintain forward motion." Down came a length of wire cable with a big hook on the end, the tractor was started up, and the Magnette made a " smooth, silent passage " to the summit, and was there pushed on to the grass and pathetically abandoned.

The passenger was again my fiancée-to-be. Something had to be done ; the night had to be spent somewhere. I returned down the hill on foot. Fortune was with me. I ran into Cecil Evans and Keith Steadman, from Bristol. They inquired why I had failed on the hill, and I told them how the clutch had been slipping all the way from Taunton. Evans had his Magnette parked near the foot of the hill and kindly offered to drive round to the top of the hill (he said he knew a way round) and tow my damaged car back to " civilisation." We got the car back into Wadebridge, and delivered it into the hands of the local garage. Two forlorn and very weary people then set off on foot to fix accommodation, at least for that night, and maybe one or two nights. At the " Molesworth Arms " we got the last two rooms, scarcely more than attics (they had dormer windows), but there were beds in which to sleep off our weariness.

In the morning I got through on the 'phone to the " Porth-minster " at St. Ives, and got hold of John Thornley, who had gone through the trial as passenger in Toulmin's " Cream Cracker." John promised to come up and rescue us, and see what could be done with the car. Just as we were finishing lunch, Crawford's and Toulmin's M.G.s arrived, together with a Morris Twelve saloon, which had been driven through the trial by Philip Potter, a friend of Toulmin's, and frequently his passenger on events. Potter was our rescuer. The rear seats of the Morris were unoccupied and he had come along, with the two M.G.s, to take my fiancée and myself through to Exeter. Thornley had a look at my car, which the garage had already begun to dismantle, and after getting a few more bits to pieces, announced that nothing could possibly be done with it until he was able to get back to the M.G. works and authorise the dispatch of a number of new parts.

" Every cloud has a silver lining." Certainly things might have been a heap worse : in fact, having served me the dirty trick of the actual breakdown, it seemed that fate was then pre-pared to play all my way. When the proprietor of the garage, of whom I cannot speak too highly, learned that my home was in Birmingham, he told me that he regularly visited Oxford, and that if I liked, when the car was ready for the road again, he would drive up to Oxford in it, and arrange to meet me there. Naturally I jumped at the idea. My fiancée's parents were spending the Easter holiday at Weston-super-Mare, so we passed the Sunday night at the Rougemont at Exeter, whence we were so kindly transported by Philip Potter in the Morris, and were collected by my fiancée's sister's husband and taken on to Weston the next morning. Variety is the spice of life.

In due course I heard from Wadebridge that the car was ready for the road again, and, shortly after, I took possession of it in Oxford, and brought it home, just in time for the M.G. Car Club's Abingdon Trial.

The " Abingdon " route started, as was now customary, with a " double-garaging " test in the grounds at the M.G. works. This was one of the many varieties of special or tie-deciding tests. Trestles and light barriers were placed to represent two garages side by side. The competitor accelerated to them, from a line a little way off, and had to enter one garage forwards and the adjacent garage in reverse, thereafter returning to the starting-point, a time being taken for the complete manœuvre. Penalty was also exacted for fouling any of the barriers or trestles forming the garages.

Thereafter the route led out into the Cotswolds, taking in the inevitable Nailsworth Ladder. A bunch of my friends were standing on the left of the hill, just by the famous bump. As the Magnette, properly in form again, came charging over the bumps, I lifted a hand from the wheel to wave to them—and, with a rending crack, the crown-wheel stripped ! It was not until after the Magnette had been man-handled clear of the fairway that I suddenly discovered that, on the opposite side of the track, was a small picnic party complete with hamper, consisting of Mr. and Mrs. Kimber and their daughter Betty !

Rather than give one of my friends the unenviable task of towing the Magnette all the way home to Birmingham, I decided that the best thing to do was to waylay the " Musketeer " boys as they came up to the hill, beg, borrow, or steal one of their spare differential units, and fix up my own car on the spot. There are, of course, other ways of spending a sunny Saturday afternoon, but. . . . The job was through for tea-time, but I had been having some very black thoughts while I was at work. I was being forced, very reluctantly, to realize that a halt would have to be called. The " Land's End " debacle had set me back the better part of £30. I was still staggering under the blow : now here was further trouble. I called a halt, albeit with a very heavy heart.

Even at that I could not keep away altogether. I went down to Camberley Heath and saw Allard win the Lawrence Cup Trial, and up to Blackpool, with Frank Kemp, to help Maurice Toulmin with the Blackpool Rally.

The Rally type of event closely resembled the very early trials of the days before the introduction of the standing-start, non-stop hill, and the mileage covered was one of the principal features, up to 1000 in some of the big rallies. The finish was usually at a leading seaside resort or spa town, where would be staged several " against-the-watch " tests, with penalties for error in carrying them out, such as fouling barriers or crossing artificial boundaries, rather than for exceeding a bogey time.

The onlooker sees most of the game. From my " ring-side " seat I followed the fortunes and misfortunes of those who had been my fellow-competitors. I realized that J. E. S. Jones's old J2 M.G. was appearing prominently in trials again, driven by P. S. Flower. I learned that Flower had not the use of his legs, the result of a tree-climbing accident when a boy, and the M.G. had been fitted up with special hand-controls. Flower was not new to trials, but his previous mount, one of the older " F "-type Magnas, had become rather outmoded as trials became ever more severe. With the purchase of the J2, Flower went straight into the front rank of trials drivers.

I observed that nearly every driver was following Macdermid's famous slogan, " It's better blown," superchargers being very much the " fashion."

I watched the " Musketeer " and " Cracker " boys go steadily from strength to strength, ever pursued by the Allard Special.

I saw that new names were appearing regularly in results lists. I discovered that the $1\frac{1}{2}$-litre Singer, with which W. C. Butler, of Derby, was gathering in awards, was Patrick's old car, Patrick no longer making regular appearances in trials. Another $1\frac{1}{2}$-litre Singer was bringing success for Geoffrey Taylor, who hailed from Stourbridge. Taylor, later, attempted to " out-do " Onslow Bartlett's incredible old " M "-type Midget (which had won the " Abingdon " hands down) with a " special " consisting mainly of bull-nosed Cowley, almost devoid of body. I was now frequently meeting in results lists the name of T. C. Wise, whom

I had first met when we had been paired together in the Sunbac
v. Lancs and Cheshire match trial. Wise was now running in a
lot of southern events.

Gone, too, were the days when it seemed that every leading
driver was mounted either on an M.G. or a Singer. In addition
to the Frazer-Nash-B.M.W.s, which had shown themselves
peculiarly suited to trials conditions from their very first appearance, and the special open-bodied Ford V8's, out of which
had been born the Allard, 1936 brought us the very attractive
little 995 c.c., sports Ballila Fiats. Westwood, of the white Singer
team, formed a trio of the new Fiats, with Dick Sanford and
Stanley Tett, his place in the white Singer team being filled by
Godfrey Imhof. C. G. Fitt was now driving one of the B.M.W.s,
and Mrs. Moss had an altogether original mount, so far as trials
were concerned, in the shape of a Marendaz Special.

At last my good resolution could be maintained no longer.
The desire to drive in competition once more proved irresistible,
and I entered for the " Barnstaple." The " Barnstaple " takes
place, by long-established tradition, on August Bank Holiday
Saturday, and I hope that I shall not offend the susceptibilities
of the Mid-Surrey Automobile Club if I say that I, personally,
have always looked upon the " Barnstaple " more in the light of
a first-class excuse for spending the August week-end in North
Devon than as a particularly serious trial. Not that I competed
in the " Barnstaple " for that reason alone : it was always a
jolly little event, and takes in the most delightful scenery. On
this occasion there had been quite a deal of wet weather in
advance of the event, and we were not allowed, by the regulations,
to use competition tyres.

By way of Doverhay and Edbrooke (where ten failed) and a
double stop-and-go test on Wellshead, the route led to a new
hill, Southern Wood, which is in the Oare Valley. This was the
most difficult hill, and although there were only the same number
of failures as at Edbrooke, there were a number of " only justs."

Lyn hairpin followed, and then Beggar's Roost, and finally
Kipscombe. Kipscombe was especially easy, but I obtained, as
I thought, a surprising amount of wheelspin getting away from
the line on this hill. It was only afterwards I realized that what
I had taken for wheelspin had been the first symptoms of a
further bout of clutch trouble. This reached its climax in the
next event in which I ran the Magnette, the Singer Motor-Car

Club's Sporting Half-Day Trial, finishing up at Rushmere.
Clutch slip set in to such an extent that on two of the hills the
Magnette could not be got off the starting-line.

So once again, fearful of another " Land's End " break-up,
I decided that withdrawal, at any rate for a period, from active
competition was the only course to pursue. I knew that, so long
as I retained the Magnette, the urge to run it in trials again would
prove too persistent to be denied, and so I decided that old
friends must part. I arranged to trade it in against one of the
new, series " T," 1292 c.c., 10 h.p. M.G. Midgets, which had
superseded the 8 h.p. " PA " and the 9 h.p. " PB " models in the
summer.

CHAPTER VI

" *Cream Cracker* "

DIEHARD M.G. enthusiasts had eyed the new Midget a bit askance ; I must admit that I had done so myself. One looked suspiciously at the little 9-inch diameter brake-drums, and scratched one's head a bit about the push-rod engine with the dynamo *on the side*. When I first started to open up, after the initial running-in period, I began to have visions of my first J2 : valve springs went off pop all over the place with persistent regularity. Stronger and yet stronger springs were tried, until at last the trouble was completely scotched with triple valve springs. Thereafter, provided one avoided an alarming period, somewhere between 75 and 80, which almost snatched the steering-wheel out of your hands, the expected brand of " safety fast " motoring could be comfortably indulged in.

The Light Car Club's Buxton–Buxton Trial and my birthday fell on the same day, Sunday, October 4th, so I decided to mark the occasion by arranging to go along to Buxton to have a first outing in one of the 1936 " Cream Cracker " cars, as passenger with Crawford. It was an exhilarating experience. At first the noise was a little disconcerting, because, to take care of the very high performance of the supercharged engines, all the " Cracker " and " Musketeer " cars had been equipped with new crown-wheels and pinions, having straight-cut teeth instead of the conventional spiral-bevel. The clatter of straight-cut gears has to be experienced ; it cannot be imagined. This was the only discordant note, the subdued whine of the " blower " being really pleasing. There was a lovely " all-in-one-piece " feeling about these little cars. The rear suspension was taken care of by telecontrol shock absorbers, instantly adjustable by a handle under the instrument panel, and at the front there were, in addition to the normal pair of friction-type shockers, a pair of the small hydraulic pattern. The actual performance of these grand little cars must still be so well remembered as to need no further embellishment from me, and, in any case, the long list of successes standing to their credit speaks more eloquently of their capabilities than any mere words. The " Crackers " were ace-high in the trials world at this time, so that, at first, I refused to believe Crawford when he intimated to me that the cars might soon come into the open market for general purchase.

After a little thought I realized that, with the introduction of the series " T " Midgets, the " PBs " were no longer the current production type, and that a team of the series " T " would have to come into being. Crawford said he thought I ought to try to buy one of the " Cracker " cars—he could not take seriously my avowed intention to stay out of trials. I said that if I knew what to use for money I would not hesitate to try to obtain one of the cars. Even so, I made a few inquiries down at Abingdon, and was told that, if the cars were released, they would be already forsworn, so that was that.

On October 22nd I attended another very successful and extremely enjoyable M.G. Car Club Show-Time Dinner-Dance, again at the Park Lane Hotel, and again with Lord Nuffield in the chair, and managed a visit to the Motor Show also.

Within a few days I was at another club dinner (or rather supper), but in quite different circumstances. The committee of the Midland Centre of the Club, on which I was still happily serving, threw a party at the King's Head at Aston Cantlow. Most Midlands folks know this pub pretty well, but if, in your travels, you have not yet made its acquaintance, that is an error which you must rectify so soon as conditions permit. This party proved to be the first of a tremendously successful series of club evenings. After supper " Curly " Squire (" borrowed " from Sunbac) played the piano, and was backed up by my business partner, Leonard Simmons, violin and " Swannee " whistle, Sydney Ison, saxophone, and myself on drums. It was at this party that I first heard Pat Reynolds tell his all-time classic about the prize-winning baby and the father with an impediment in his speech. Reynolds, whose line of business is insulation, and who plays a good game of both rugby football and water-polo, is well known in the Midlands. You may know Reynolds, but not the baby story. If so, you must have it told to you.

Much sterner stuff followed—I passengered Crawford again, this time in the " Experts." We went down to Dunster on Friday evening, and stayed the night at the old " Luttrell Arms." I woke during the night and heard it raining heavens hard, and it was still drizzling a little in the morning. The organizers had gone to the opposite extreme this year, not only competition tyres, blowers, and locked differentials being allowed, but even the use of chains was permitted. Intending competitors were warned, however, that it would be tough.

The first non-stop hill, Ashwell, also known under the alternative name of Cutcombe, proved little more than an appetizer, and the Kershams, too, seemed rather to have lost their sting. Was it going to be so tough ?

" What happens next ? "

" Er—straight on to Couple Cross, and—oh ! Widlake next, and Cloutsham ! "

Widlake was in form, but so were Crawford and the " Cracker," so that, for the first time, I saw the top of the hill. It was an exciting, not to say breath-taking, few moments. I kept as far to my side of the car as was possible, to avoid Crawford's left elbow, almost dug my feet into the floorboards and braced myself with both hands. The little car rocketed to the top in a series of leaps and slides. If you have never had the experience, I can assure you that 20–25 m.p.h. up Widlake is every bit as thrilling as 120 m.p.h. on Brooklands.

Crawford confided to me that he had never yet climbed Cloutsham non-stop. " The better the day, the better the deed." This being the Experts Trial, it seemed to me a suitable occasion to lay the Cloutsham bogey. Crawford thought so too, and bounced the " Cracker " over Cloutsham's boulders and rock outcrop to pass the " Observed Section Ends " notice non-stop. Yealscombe should have come next, but the torrential rain overnight had caused the Exe, which you will remember has to be forded to reach the foot of the hill, to rise in flood, and when our car arrived at the hill, one of the official cars, Michael May's Alvis, I believe, was actually stuck in the river, and competitors were diverted to Downscombe.

Downscombe was terribly rough, rather on the lines of the Derbyshire hills, all rocks and not much gradient, so that car and crew were terribly shaken up.

A stretch of main road followed, and, at Simonsbath, we picked up the " Land's End " route for a mile or so. We turned away at a point known as Blue Gate, and began to descend towards the River Barle. Suddenly the road turned a little left and dipped sharply. As we came over the crest of this dip the river lay straight before us, and floating, so it seemed, in the river was Miss E. V. Watson's Frazer-Nash-B.M.W.

1936 " GLOUCESTER "—C. DENNIS BUCKLEY (" GRASSHOPPER " AUSTIN)
CLIMBING NAILSWORTH LADDER

Photo : "The Motor"

1936 "GLOUCESTER"—R. A. MACDERMID OVERTURNS IN REVERSING DOWN MIDDLE DRAG

The Barle was in flood from the overnight rain, and quite what prompted Miss Watson to attempt what was to me, even without the evidence of the stranded car, an impossible crossing, was never really explained. A picture of the scene, as Crawford and I saw it, is before me. Although the B.M.W. is only a short way from the water's edge, the wheels are entirely under water, and Miss Watson and her girl passenger are perched on the back of the body, scarcely keeping their feet out of the water.

Toulmin and Jones joined us. A rope was found, somebody, most fortunately, had a pair of waders, and it was decided to wade into the water, get a line on the B.M.W., and endeavour to tow it out backwards. Toulmin reversed his car down to the water's edge, the line was made firm between the B.M.W. and the M.G., and Toulmin revved up and engaged the clutch. Despite being shod with competition tryes, the M.G.'s driving-wheels spun furiously in the loose wet gravel at the water's edge, and the B.M.W. did not move. Crawford's car was roped in tandem with Toulmin's ; at a signal both drivers started off together, and after an anxious moment, the B.M.W. came slowly out of the river, shedding water like a dog shaking itself after a swim.

John Thornley, service manager at M.G., was riding with Toulmin, and, under his directions, the vital parts of the B.M.W. were dismantled and dried out, while Miss Watson and her passenger salvaged sodden packets of sandwiches and saturated personal belongings. Then came the great moment when it was decided to see if the B.M.W.'s engine could be started up. After a few gurglings and grunts, the engine suddenly sprang into life, water shot out of the exhaust-pipe in a solid stream, but it kept going, and Miss Watson drove it back to Dunster.

Meanwhile there had been a hurried consultation amongst the organizers and it was decided that, although Cowcastle, the hill immediately across the river, would have to be abandoned, it was possible to redirect competitors to enable them to get round to Picked Stones, the second of the special new hills. If you have not driven or ridden in an Experts Trial, probably Picked Stones is unfamiliar to you. From Picked Stones Farm, which is marked fairly clearly on a 1-inch scale Ordnance Survey map, south-east of Simonsbath, there is a vaguely discernible sheep-track on the side of a hill, leading down to the crossing of a little tributary of the Barle. Here is the first obstacle. The

banks on either side of the stream are steep, so that your car
drops steeply into the stream and has to climb sharply out on the
other side, then being faced with the main part of the hill, consisting of a climbing right-hand turn on grass, at once followed
by a very sharp left-hand hairpin, still on grass, and so narrow
that one reverse was permitted—definitely a " driver's hill," the
non-stop section starting before the stream.

I remember I twisted in my seat and faced backwards as the
M.G.'s bonnet dipped sharply to the stream. For a second or
two there was water, water everywhere, and then we were away,
spinning furiously on the wet grass, but keeping going, and
climbed to the hairpin. Crawford was having a grand run, and
that evening, at the " Luttrell Arms," we learned that he had
"won the race " and, in addition, the " Crackers " had taken the
team prize. What a day out !

At this stage I was already toying with the idea of putting my
series " T " Midget into a couple of trials (not, of course, of the
" Experts " calibre) and seeing just how it did pan out.

It was as observer, though, that I went again to Buxton for
the Motor-Cycling Club's One-Day Sporting Trial. But on the
Sunday morning, before returning home, I decided to take the
" T " round to Bamford Clough. I met with small fortune ;
three completely fruitless attempts were made on the hill, none
getting even half-way up. It was being noised around, already,
that the " Cracker " boys were to have series " T " cars, instead
of the blown " PBs," and I went back to Buxton, found Crawford,
and related to him the details of my Bamford Clough failures.
He told me that he himself would be along there later. John
Thornley had come up specially from Abingdon, with a slightly
modified car, and a number of the drivers were going to try it
out in the district, and see if it could be licked into shape for
serious competition work. Soon afterwards Crawford saw me
again, and I heard that this car had climbed Bamford and given
a satisfactory account of itself altogether. It was only a good
deal later still that I learned the details of the car's equipment,
and in due course a sort of set schedule of " modification " for
trials purposes was listed by M.G., and made available, at a
very reasonable figure, to any series " T " owner.

On Saturday, November 14th, I took the series " T " car into
its first trial, the Bristol Motor Cycle and Light Car Club's
Fedden Trophy Trial. Frankly, its performance exceeded my

expectations, considering it was pulling a bottom gear ratio of
16·47 : 1. I wondered if this would prove too high to get away
on Nailsworth Ladder, but it was not, and Hodgecombe, too,
was successfully climbed. Hodgecombe was a new hill, and a
very good one, difficult, fair, and non-damaging. It was at the
second of the new hills introduced in this event, Middle Drag,
that the car's limitations, at any rate in its standard form, were
shown up. Middle Drag proved, both in this event and again
in the " Gloucester," a few weeks later, to be a very difficult
hill, but the series " T " failed here in the " Fedden " for sheer
lack of power to pull its 16·1 bottom gear, even before the difficult
part of the hill was reached.

Sunbac's Shell Cup Trial, the following week-end, was more
to the " T's " liking. In Worcestershire the Middle Drags and
Widlakes do not abound, and Sunbac provides the afternoon's
fun and games mainly through cunningly sited re-starts and
"tight" timed tests. Sunbac had a particular flair for this style of
event, which, in less-experienced hands, might easily have been
something of an anti-climax for drivers fresh from " horrors "
such as Picked Stones and Middle Drag. I can pay Sunbac no
better compliment than to say that, although the " Shell " was
a local event, for club members only, it always enjoyed the
support of the leading drivers. H. L. Hadley won the Cup, with
one of the " Grasshopper " Austins, closely chased home by
N. V. Terry with the B.M.W. The series " T " pulled in its
first award.

For the next week-end there was scheduled the M.G. Car
Club's Down-Stage dinner, this time to be held in the big restaurant
at the Regent's Park Zoo. As this meant staying the night in or
near London, I decided to make a week-end of it and go on, on
the Sunday morning, to the Kentish Border Car Club's trial. I
had a grand week-end.

The " down-stage " was even more hilarious than before,
and it is a fact that at one time the restaurant manager was on
the point of sending for the police, misinterpreting an excess of
high spirits as a wilful intent to do harm, and most definitely the
party was never at any time out of hand. The street musicians
were in attendance again, now supported by a number of theatre-
queue entertainers, who sang, tore paper, rattled spoons, and
generally helped the evening along. The fireworks, still mainly
of the type intended for outdoor use, were on a much more

ambitious scale. Somebody let off a thunder-flash under my chair, and I remember Mr. Kimber being presented with a trombone, on which he actually played a few notes.

I had not been in Kent for some time and nearly all of the hills used in the trial on the Sunday were new to me. I failed Shrubbs Wood hairpin, but surprisingly the M.G. climbed Stowting, also justifying those " comic little hydraulic brakes," which had been the subject of much comment, by making best performance in the braking test. This event gave me a new angle on the suitability of Kent as " trials country."

It was in this event that I first got on to terms of personal friendship with W. J. (" Dickie ") Green, laying the basis of a friendship which ripened to the extent that, within eighteen months of my first getting to know him, he was to fill the rôle of " best man " at my wedding. I had been aware of a new name appearing regularly high up in trials results lists for some time past, and, of course, of the fact that Green was driving an M.G., this providing a basis on which to get acquainted. I found that the M.G., a 939 c.c. " PB " Midget, was Marshall supercharged, and also had the light J2 mudguards.

Meanwhile, behind the scenes in the trials world, things had been going on. In an article in *The Autocar*, November 20th, 1942, one of a series reviewing the trials days, I summed up the position very roughly in these words :

" . . . It was assumed, whether rightly or wrongly I will not discuss, that certain consistently successful cars and drivers were directly works supported, having available to them, without any worry about the £ s. d. angle, every possible facility for success in competition. With the wealth of special equipment available, so the argument continued, these cars became such efficient machines that, to give them ' a run for their money,' trials courses of exceptional severity were having to be devised, so that time and again there were sections where, for the most part, only certain of the specialized cars climbed, and the poor ' private owner,' to whom, presumably, this range of highly specialized equipment was neither readily nor cheaply available, was considered to be providing merely the unrewarded background against which the ' works ' drivers did their stuff.

" Carried to its logical conclusion, the position appeared to be that trials would become—and in fact, in some people's opinion, already were—the playground of but a selected handful of drivers. Such an outlook was not to the liking of a number of organizers nor to that of certain drivers. That, perhaps, is not all the story, but is sufficient for present purposes . . . when the North-West London Motor Club issued the regulations for their annual North Devon team trial competitors were required to sign a declaration that the cars they would drive were their own property, bought and paid for, and as a further guarantee of their *bona fides*, had to be prepared to sell their cars at the conclusion of the event, at current market value, to whomsoever should be interested in purchasing them."

The regulations for the "Gloucester" went further. In addition to the "Selling-Plate" clause, as it came to be known, there was a regulation calling for oil, water, and petrol filler-caps to be sealed at the start, and to be opened for replenishment only at the breakfast stop, and for bonnets to be locked. Frankly the regulations were not popular. I think the feelings of "the boys" were summed up pretty neatly by F. L. M. Harris, in *The Sports Car* (November 1936). He said :

". . . The 'selling-plate' idea will not and cannot accomplish whatever end is desired—for an excellent reason. It is a horse-racing idea, and when a stallion or a mare wins an important race it can go to a stud farm and then earn money for its owner for many years to come. A car is an entirely different proposition. Aside from the fact that it cannot reproduce its species, its market value is nowhere near its catalogue price. . . . And, in any case, penalizing the successful can never prove to be a popular policy. If everyone concerned with the organization of trials had pursued such a policy since they first began, where would the clubs be now ? I suggest that it is principally the few spectacular figures in the trials game who keep the sport alive and vigorous."

The regulations, naturally, had considerable effect on the "Gloucester" entry. Of the "Musketeer" team, only Macdermid competed, driving his 1935, original "Cream Cracker" Midget. Crawford entered his black "N" Magnette, the engine now Marshall supercharged, Jones drove his unblown "PB," Toulmin was not present. Boughton brought his everyday saloon Triumph, instead of the two-seater competition car, with Alf Langley as passenger. There were other changes of cars and drivers, not so directly attributable to the regulations. The Ruddy Singer team having disbanded, Dave Harris was now doing his stuff with an "N" Magnette, supercharged, of course, while Imhof, erstwhile Singer driver, came to the start with the very series T.M.G. that had been tried out at Buxton, the day after the M.C.C. One-Day Sporting, when I could not get my " T " up Bamford.

I competed in the " Gloucester " on Toulmin's 1936 " Cream Cracker " M.G., JB 7521. On the Monday morning immediately preceding the trial there arrived from Abingdon a letter advising me that one of the " Cream Cracker " cars could be made available to me after all. I was on the telephone at once. Could I take immediate possession ? Could I run it in the " Gloucester " ? Yes, the car was all set to take straight into a trial. Well, that was all right, but there remained the problem of finding £200, the figure at which the car was offered to me. I haggled ; we compromised at £180. It made no difference : I hadn't got £180 either. Of course, I had got the series " T," but an immediate sale on that, so soon after purchase, would involve maximum depreciation. It seemed more my father's type of problem, and on Wednesday I went down to Abingdon with his cheque and collected the car, to find that the particular car being released to me was the one Toulmin always drove.

The rear axle had the differential lock in position, not allowed by the " Gloucester " regulations, but I had expected this and had made preparations to get the lock removed in time. This was possible through the good graces of Ted Lloyd-Jones, to whose garage in Shirley, Birmingham, there came, over the years, nearly all of the Midlands drivers' cars, and many from farther afield too. Lloyd-Jones had been at the same school as myself, though he left the term before I started, was apprenticed at P. J. Evans Ltd. when they held the M.G. agency, and later opened his own establishment.

The sump oil-level was low when I got back to Birmingham from Abingdon. I had not checked it before leaving the works, so, of course, the sump might not have been full when I started from M.G.'s. Unfortunately, the run down to the " Spider's Web," on London's Watford by-pass, for the start of the " Gloucester " on Friday evening, showed me otherwise. The engine was using quite a drop of oil. I began to wonder about those sealed filler-caps and locked bonnets.

Worse followed. Within a few miles of the start the engine suddenly started to cut out above 4500 revolutions, and then the instrument-panel gauge recording the pressure in the telecontrol rear shock absorbers fell steadily away, and it was not a case of a faulty gauge. The outlook was black. The " Cracker " cars had a very definite reputation. I felt a certain responsibility to uphold it, but with only " four, five " attainable. . . .

But the cup of sorrow was to be filled to the brim, as they say in the novels. I have always suffered a type of nervous anxiety which has its physical form in acute nausea and " fluttering " of the tummy, and pops up at all sorts of inconvenient moments. It popped up at the breakfast stop in acute form. I huddled in my car in " The Plough " yard after breakfast, in the dark and cold, wondering Oh ! death where is thy sting ! I was of two minds whether to continue the trial. I did go on, more or less in a state of coma, completed the downhill braking-test on Ferriscourt and the immediately following double stop-and-go test up Bismore, and then woke up with a jerk. The engine had not been touched because of the locked bonnet, yet there had not been a trace of a misfire or cut-out on Bismore and, by the very nature of the test, the engine had been forced pretty well to its limit. I was never able to explain this phenomenon, and exactly the same thing happened on the " Exeter " soon afterwards.

By way of the non-stop hills Quarhouse, Ham Mill, and Old Hollow, the trial arrived at Middle Drag. To those of us who had competed in the " Fedden " it was no surprise to find that failures were to be the order of the day at Middle Drag. Macdermid got away in front of me. The M.G.'s exhaust note faded away up the hill, and a long wait followed. I got out of my car and started to walk up the hill, and, to my great surprise, I found Macdermid and his passenger, assisted by three officials of the club and the arm of the law, putting the old " Cracker " back on to its four wheels. Macdermid had failed on the hill, and, in reversing back, had slewed up the greasy bank at the side of the track and the M.G. had gone over on its side. Any doubts that might still have lingered about my car's proposed behaviour that day were finally laid at Middle Drag. The little car went hurtling to the summit in that confidence-inspiring manner that I had experienced with Crawford's car when I rode with him in the " Experts."

From Middle Drag we went to the other " Fedden " hill, Hodgecombe. Hodgecombe wet was an utterly different proposition to what it had been in the " Fedden," as most competitors found out. I had a terrific struggle, and, while it may take some believing, I know definitely that the "Cracker" came much nearer to failure at Hodgecombe than at Juniper. Curiously, and I must ask you to believe that I am not just shooting a line, I never felt like failing on Juniper, even though it was so difficult that only four competitors were successful—Miss Goodban, Macdermid, Flower, and myself. I cannot explain it. I did not expect to climb, the less so when Harold Avery, who was in charge of the hill, told me that Allard had failed.

Subsequently, my ex-"Cream Cracker" car failed on Juniper several times, but that day it is a fact that I did not have an anxious moment : the car just simply motored up—why, I cannot tell you. But at Hodgecombe my heart was in my mouth : I snap-changed up and down, up and down, expecting to come to a standstill at any moment. I rarely remember again experiencing wheelspin to such a degree without actually failing (*i.e.* coming to a standstill).

Coming away from Juniper, I thought I could smell burning, something more pungent, it seemed, than the quickly recognized aroma of mud cooking on the red-hot silencer and exhaust-pipe. I was just about to broach the matter to my passenger when smoke rose alarmingly between his legs. We abandoned ship hurriedly, grabbed handfuls of wet grass and soaked earth from the roadside, and smothered the smouldering floorboards. We could then see that what had happened was that the silencer had been bumped up, probably somewhere like Ham Mill, so that it had been pressing against the floorboards, and had got so hot coming up Juniper, flat-out in bottom gear, that it had set the floorboards alight. There was a hole about 4 inches by 2 inches.

Next excitement was the timed climb up Ferriscourt. You remember Ferris, of course, with its sharp, right-hand corner near the bottom, and a turn back to the left higher up. I had changed up, and was pushing the revolution counter well round in second when I reached the corner. There was an exciting moment, and I was glad that the passenger and I had looked at the rear shockers and found that they could be tightened up by hand, just like ordinary friction shock absorbers. As to the oil position, I could only take heart from the continued steadiness of the oil-pressure gauge. Reverse gear was no longer obtainable, as I had found out when I overshot a corner and the passenger and I had to push the wretched car backwards. But the thing was that no failure had been recorded so far, and, after those black beginnings, the silver lining was coming through ever more brightly. Only Station and Nailsworth still had to be climbed. I had to smile at the report which said that I climbed Nailsworth " in a brisk and lively " manner.

I knew that it had been a difficult " Gloucester," but it was not until W. J. B. Richardson, who had been acting clerk-of-the-course, came and talked with Crawford and myself over our lunch at " The Bear " that I began to realize that it had been so difficult that only Miss Goodban, with her B.M.W., and myself were without fault. The " Cracker " beat the B.M.W. on the timed tests, but Miss Goodban had her compensation in qualifying for a Gloucester Goblet. May I go that extra paragraph and give the full results ?

The Gloucester Cup.—C. A. N. May (939 c.c. M.G. s/c).
President's Trophy.—P. S. Flower (847 c.c. M.G.).
North-West London Cup.—Miss P. D. Goodban (1991 c.c. B.M.W.).
Thomas Challenge Cup.—S. H. Allard (3622 c.c. Allard).
Committee Cup.—A. G. Imhof (1292 c.c. M.G.).
Second-Class Awards.—R. A. Macdermid (M.G.) ; D. E. Harris (M.G.) ; H. K. Crawford (M.G.) ; H. G. Symmons (B.M.W.).
Third-Class Awards.—E. H. Goodenough (M.G.) ; G. T. I. Taylor (Singer) ; C. M. Anthony (Aston-Martin) ; N. V. Terry (B.M.W.) ; C. G. Fitt (B.M.W.) ; A. Eadon (Singer) ; R. Lloyd (M.G.) ; M. H. Lawson (Singer) ; L. E. C. Hall (Singer).
Team Award.—May, Crawford, C. D. Buckley (Austin).

Rather interesting reading ; Flower and Allard high in the list as was now customary, the new series " T " winning its spurs, in Imhof's hands, and practically all of the other awards going to the " regulars." Such were the results of the selling-plate, sealed-fillers, locked-bonnets " Gloucester."

CHAPTER VII

1937

TOULMIN, Crawford, and Jones had their new series " T " Midgets for the " Exeter." Painted in the brown and cream of Abingdon, and with the now inevitable J2 mudguards and the big-section rear tyres, the three new " Cream Cracker " cars certainly looked workmanlike. To refresh your memory, the engines had the compression-ratios raised from standard 6·5 : 1 to 7·5 : 1, there were new " bits " in the gear-boxes, giving first and second gears of 19·5 : 1 and 11·56 : 1 respectively, instead of the standard 16·47 and 9·95, and the bodies and bonnets were of aluminium, to save weight.

Their début was nearly marred when Crawford's car sustained damage to the sump, which had to be plugged with chewing-gum, and subsequently the cars were fitted with pressed-steel sumps instead of the more vulnerable cast-aluminium.

Windout, Fingle Bridge, Simms, Pin Hill (re-start), and Meerhay were the " Exeter " hills. It was a good, fair trial, but not in the same street with the " Land's End," and after Simms interest begins to wane. I found it terribly difficult to keep awake on the last stretch from Meerhay to Blandford. One was glad to see Simms getting back to form, with 165 failures.

There had been some speculation as to what cars would be driven by the " Musketeer " boys in the new year, since it was known that they, too, were to have a change of vehicle, and the new 1½-litre M.G., with its bigger chassis, did not seem to lend itself to conversion into a trials machine. When the new cars had their first airing, in the Margate and District Club's Wye Cup Trial, they were found to be identical with the new " Cream Cracker " cars, distinguished only by their being painted bright red. The début was an auspicious one, Bastock's car winning the Wye Cup, Langley's car the Committee Cup, and the team award being taken.

For the " Colmore," Sunbac were reintroducing Leckhampton, and with Juniper and new Kineton figuring on the route card also, it was obviously going to be a stiff event. Sunbac had a grand idea for minimizing delay. Some of the hills lay north of Cheltenham, some south, so that the course was devised in two loops, making a very rough figure of eight, with Cheltenham in the centre. While half the entry was tackling the northern hill, the remainder were on the southern loop.

I went out on the southern loop first, and was at once faced with Leckhampton. Rather to my surprise the ex-" Cracker " failed within a few yards of the start, a mishap straightway repeated at Juniper. This was a terrible beginning. Then it rained in torrents, just like the 1936 " Colmore." Waiting to get away in the timed climb up Syde, the rain seemed to come completely horizontal across the hill, and it was bitterly cold into the bargain. Within a few yards of the finishing-line the M.G.'s engine cut out dead. In a deluge of rain I endeavoured to find a reason. I got as far as determining that it was ignition, not petrol, when Alf Langley came along and, taking pity on me, took the M.G. in tow and got me back on to the main road, to where I could coast down the hill into Cheltenham.

Back at " The Plough," over tea and during the evening, I had to learn the story of the " Colmore " at second hand. Juniper and Leckhampton had taken heavy toll, fifteen climbing the former only, and seventeen managing Leckhampton non-stop. I was intrigued to hear that one competitor who had been successful on both hills was Lloyd-Jones, taking a day off from mending other people's cars to air his " Triangle Special." On various visits to his garage I had seen the " Special " come into being. It had started life as a supercharged, hyper-Lea-Francis. The chassis had been both shortened and narrowed, the radiator lowered, and the body was from a " K3 " racing M.G., actually R. G. Horton's, discarded when this driver had a single-seater body fitted for his Brooklands records. The rear-axle assembly, if I remember rightly, was mainly Sunbeam.

Allard won the Colmore Trophy ; Buckley, Bastock, and R. M. Andrews collecting the other cups. Andrews had purchased one of the " P " type Midgets which had originally run at Le Mans in 1935, sponsored by G. E. T. Eyston and driven in turns by the six girls who were dubbed " The Dancing Daughters." It was now fitted with a " PB " engine, supercharged and painted in the chocolate and cream Abingdon colours. Another " car with a history " in the " Colmore " was a special-bodied, 1½-litre Singer, originally devised for Miss Astbury to drive in long-distance rallies, the body being arranged to enable the second driver to lie out full length to get a sleep between driving spells. K. C. Delingpole had taken this car over. I had met Delingpole while I had my Magnette, at which time he was driving one also, and we were to become the closest of friends.

It would seem that old trials cars, like old soldiers, never die. To take an example at random, consider Macdermid's original " Cream Cracker " M.G. Midget, JB 3639. This car was first registered as an 847 c.c. " P "-type Midget in the early spring of 1934, and driven in event after event throughout that year, usually successfully. At the year's end it went back to Abingdon, and emerged for the " Exeter," considerably modified, repainted chocolate and cream, and bearing on the bonnet, for the first time, the name " Cream Cracker." In the spring a Centric supercharger was fitted. The car went from success to success, winning, among many other events, the very difficult and hard-fought Brighton–Beer Trial of 1935. When Macdermid took over one of the " Musketeer " Magnettes, the Midget went into semi-retirement, but was brought out at intervals during 1936. I remember it ran in the " Lawrence," and Macdermid drove it again in the 1936 " Gloucester," as described a few pages back. In due course Macdermid parted with it, and shortly afterwards it turned up in Scotland, in the hands of E. R. Herrald, and started all over again.

For the Coventry Cup Trial the North-West London Motor Club again experimented. Competitors were divided into two classes, for standard and non-standard cars, even the use of slightly oversize tyres rendering a car non-standard. In neither section was the use of competition tyres permitted. The route was set in the Surrey hills, starting from the Royal Huts Hotel at Hindhead.

There was snow on the way down to the start, on the Friday evening, the tail-end of the journey being most uncomfortable. In the morning we woke to a white world, a thick fall of snow having frozen overnight.

The event attracted but twenty-nine competitors, though undoubtedly the absence of quantity was considerably offset by the quality of the entry. The " Cream Cracker " trio was there, Welch in place of Toulmin (though not the " Musketeers "), and Green, Imhof, Flower, Lawson, Anthony, D. E. Harris, and C. G. Fitt. Crawford's car of the 1936 " Cream Cracker " team, JB 7524, was also at the start. It had been bought by John

(E. J.) Haesendonck. The car was, of course, identical with mine, and with such a mutual interest as a basis, a close friendship quickly developed between us. Miss Goodban's B.M.W., which had shared the " Gloucester " honours with me, was also at the start, but it had a new owner, L. G. Johnson.

Johnson won the Coventry Cup, and Haesendonck won the Elham Cup (best invited club member). A number of the awards were held over and their destination not made known for quite a time afterwards. Green and myself then found that, although we had almost identical cars, we had both apparently won cups, but in different classes !

All that aside, I must say that the actual event, the climbing of the hills, that is, I thoroughly enjoyed. The Surrey countryside looked utterly delightful in its mantle of white, and the snow had certainly added to the trickiness of some of the observed hills, Begley Farm in particular. Abster's Hollow and Untertarkham were sticky, too, so that, according to *The Motor* (March 9th, 1937), on the latter hill " C. A. N. May and J. E. S. Jones both took the bend near the bottom on two wheels."

I had not, so far, disposed of the series " T " M.G., and I made a last-minute decision to drive this in the " Land's End " instead of the ex-" Cracker," partly because I wanted to get a few jobs done on the " Cracker " and largely in deference to my fiancée, who could not accustom herself to the clatter of the straight-toothed crown-wheel in the " Cracker," even on short trials, and was not at all looking forward to having to put up with it for the six or seven hundred mile round trip to Land's End and back.

" Toughest Land's End for Years " was the headline used by *The Autocar* for their report of the event. With a 16·47 : 1 bottom gear and the engine of the series " T " M.G. in no way tuned up, every hill proved a struggle for me. Even so, it was only at the re-start at Crackington that the car failed, though it was the nearest thing ever on the top section of the " new " Bluehills.

Crackington was the high-light of the trial (shades of those North-West London Motor Club team trials, when it started life under the name of Mineshop). Car after car failed to get away ; mine never moved forward a fraction of an inch when I let the clutch in. Yet, although all three of the " Musketeer " drivers and Crawford and Jones in the " Cream Cracker " team failed, Toulmin got away, a terrific display of sheer driving ability, and so did Green on the blown " PB." The supercharged Austins, led by Dennis Buckley, were successful, as were three of the new four-wheeled Morgans, one driven by H. F. S. Morgan himself. The H.R.G., too, was among the successful few ; also Butler, with the ex-Patrick, 1½-litre Singer, referred to earlier in this story. But for the majority Crackington spelt failure.

Now, I have met quite a few people who are not familiar with the H.R.G., referred to in the previous paragraph. It was a hand-built machine, produced, for the most part, in open 2/4-seater form, with a 1496 c.c., 12 h.p. engine. Named after H. R. Godfrey—the " G " of the original air-cooled, twin-cylinder G.N. cycle-car—the H.R.G. had a certain affinity, in general external appearance, with the probably better-known Frazer-Nash sports car. Unlike the Frazer-Nash, however, it employed conventional transmission instead of the chain and sprocket final drive peculiar to the Nash. The H.R.G. car scored on a very high power-to-weight ratio, and showed up well at Le Mans in the 24-hours Rudge Whitworth Cup Race.

Having retired in the 1936 " Land's End " at Hustyn, I had not had any occasion to see the extensive alterations to Bluehills Mine Hill, this being a gradient exclusive to the M.C.C. and used only in the Land's End Trial. The famous left-hand corner had been eliminated entirely, the track now going straight on up over the shoulder of the hill. At the foot an artificial " S " bend had been created, of which the second right-hand corner was extremely tricky. The hill was now divided into two sections, a re-start being staged on the upper section, just where the gradient was at its steepest.

More by luck than judgment the series " T " scraped round the bottom artificial hairpin, but on a 16 : 1 bottom gear I never entertained a hope of getting away on the steep upper section. Nevertheless I had a go for it. I banged the throttle wide open, eased in the clutch—and the car slowly edged forward, but the engine revs. literally collapsed as the drive took up. I slipped the clutch furiously, trying to " cushion " my engine revs., but still they fell off. The revolution counter needle seemed almost to swing back, falling to 1000 and then down to 800. It did not seem possible to keep the car in motion with the engine at no more than " tick-over " speed. It crawled slowly past the " Observed Section Ends " notice—and stopped !

Yes ! *The Autocar* was justified in its headline—" Toughest

Land's End for Years." Only twenty competitors received
first-class awards, and seventy-two cars retired. I think I ought
to list those twenty :

> C. D. Buckley, W. H. Scriven, J. G. Orford (blown Austins) ;
> M. S. Soames (Ford V8) ; H. G. Symmons, T. W.
> Dargue (Frazer - Nash - B.M.W.) ; A. E. S. Curtis
> (H.R.G.) ; H. I. Wilkes, A. L. Baker (M.G. Magnettes) ;
> W. J. Green (blown " PB " M.G.) ; G. Kinsey-Morgan,
> R. Bayles (M.G. Midgets) ; T. H. Jones, T. Wagner,
> H. F. S. Morgan (Morgans) ; J. F. A. Clough (Riley) ;
> G. B. Goodman, H. W. Johnson (Singer Nine Le Mans) ;
> W. C. Butler, G. L. Boughton (1½-litre Singers).

The much-coveted Team Award was secured by the three
Morgans, T. H. Jones, H. F. S. Morgan, and G. H. Goodall.

I have been looking at some old photographs. Here's one
of a relay-driving test, evidently Buxton way, from the evidence
of the dry stone walls. Behind the car just getting away from the
starting-line, is a figure in an old mackintosh and a tweed cap.
In front of him, held by a cord round his neck, is a tray, presumably holding stop-watches and report pads. That's Jack Woodhouse, secretary of the Sutton Coldfield and North Birmingham
Automobile Club—Sunbac.

Let me pay tribute to the folk who made our sport possible,
the club secretaries who organized, the enthusiastic observers who
recorded our progress on the hills, the patient stop-watch wielders,
the eagle-eyed gentry who decided if we had, or had not, crossed
line " A " with all four wheels.

He would be a brave man who would decide on which side
of the fence lay the greater degree of enthusiasm—amongst the
drivers or amongst the organizers and officials. It needs a very
special brand of enthusiasm to be stuck for more than twelve
hours on stretch on Bismore and Ferris Court clicking stop-
watches, as were Woodhouse, Mrs. S. H. Richards, and members
of the Standard Owners' Club and Sunbac, in one memorable
" Gloucester."

If you were one of those who failed on Juniper, in the 1937
Colmore Trial, you may remember the way in which advantage
was taken of the slippery nature of the surface to swing your car
right about face across the hill, and dispatch it, under its own

power, of course, down to the foot of the hill again, instead of struggling desperately to push the car to the summit. The two stalwarts who man-handled you were Ralph Gilbert, the tall, thin dark one in the roll-neck pullover, and Ken Sumner, the fair-headed, rather thick-set fellow wearing glasses. The condition of those two lads at the conclusion of the event was indescribable. That, too, is a particular brand of enthusiasm.

If I speak mainly of the men who kept Sunbac's flag flying, it is because I knew them so personally and had the opportunity, additionally, to meet them off duty, even, at the annual party, in white tie and tails. Their counterparts were to be found in most of the " live " clubs, although I must say, as a purely personal opinion, that I often felt that in Sunbac we were a shade more fortunate than average in the matter of our honorary officials.

When the decision as to the destination of a particular trophy was a matter of split seconds, no uncommon occurrence, drivers needed to have every confidence in the stop-watch clickers. I remember Macdermid, in one of his excellent monthly articles in *The Sports Car*, having a few pungent remarks to make about casual timekeepers. He was not, I am quite certain, thinking of any of Sunbac's events. Secretary Woodhouse was an accredited timekeeper to the Auto-Cycle Union, and was usually employed in that capacity on the International Six Days' Trials and many other events, and he proceeded to pass on his knowledge and the benefits of his long experience to a select band of his honorary officials, and encouraged them to something like a similar state of proficiency.

He could hardly have had a more willing or able pupil than the enthusiastic, efficient, and entirely indefatigable Mrs. S. H. Richards. The presence, at a timed test, of the familiar, dark-haired, teddy-bear-coated figure could only inspire confidence. Douglas Barwell and Curly Squire, too, were apt pupils, and tremendously energetic workers in the club's best interests. Douglas was an artist with the starter's flag also. To divert, for a moment, Squire was a tower of strength, also, on the social side of the club's activities, with his very fine rhythmic piano-playing, so that it became customary, at Sunbac dances and parties, for a part of the evening's dance music to be provided by Squire, supported by Terry Langford or myself playing drums, my partner in business, Leonard Simmons, playing his violin

Photo : "The Autocar"

1936 "GLOUCESTER"—G. W. WARBURTON (30/98 VAUXHALL) FIGHTING HARD ON JUNIPER

Photo : " The Autocar "

1937 COLMORE TROPHY TRIAL—J. DONALD BARNES (1496-c.c. SINGER)
CONQUERING JUNIPER IN POURING RAIN

and, quite often, Max Billingham, of the Singer team, on alto
saxophone. Versatile folk, these motorists.

While I am dealing in " behind-the-scenes " personalities
let me pay tribute to Bill Vincent, to whom I have already
referred earlier on as the man to whom Sunbac gave the more
" sticky " assignments, for the very good reason, of course, that
Bill was the man to see them through. Through a combination
of unhappy circumstances which even Sunbac could hardly
have provided for, there was nearly a debacle when Leckhampton
Hill was first introduced into the Colmore Trophy Trial route
in 1935. It was not used in 1936, but it figured in the route
again in 1937 with unqualified success. Vincent was the man
mainly responsible for this. Vincent had a useful right-hand
man in " Fido " Kerswell, who, in the events of other clubs, was
frequently my enthusiastic and able passenger.

While most of the Sunbac officials I have just discussed had
their counterparts in the other leading clubs, I feel that in the
person of Eric Oliver we had, perhaps, something special to
Sunbac. For one thing, Oliver was the only corporation official
I ever met who did not carry " red tape " with him. If you
lived in Birmingham, and the electric supply failed suddenly,
you would soon see a short man, in a tweed cap and an old
mackintosh, guarding a big hole in the road. That was Oliver.
After doing remarkable things, both in and out of trials, with
an oldish Clyno, Oliver then bought what must surely have
been the original Alvis car, and later turned to motor-cycle trials
again, growing never a day older through all the years.

Somewhere around the route of a Sunbac trial you would
find parked an open four-seater Armstrong car, the property of
Leslie Burnett. From Burnett one immediately goes on to think
of those other club enthusiasts, old enough by the calendar to be
one's father, but perpetually young in mind and spirit, such as
T. J. Hutton, E. G. Bromhead, and Alf Sumner (though he has
since passed on). Yes, the story of trials and of the clubs from
the organizers' point of view should surely be worth telling.

The " show-pieces " of trials organization were undoubtedly
the long-distance events of the Motor Cycling Club, under the
able direction of secretary Jackie Masters. The " Land's End,"
the " Edinburgh," and the " Exeter," both by reason of the
mileage covered and the large number of entries received
(remember the big motor-cycle entry also), could have been

very unsatisfactory affairs if there had not been a watertight organization behind them. The M.C.C. route-cards were a work of art, yet so excellent was the route-marking always that it was possible to go through without a route-card at all, except for time-keeping. I knew all the regular M.C.C. officials by sight and to talk to, but can remember few by name.

I was a member, also, of the Bristol Motor-Cycle and Light Car Club. There was some tremendous enthusiasm of entirely the right type around Bristol. The Fedden Trial, from small beginnings, quickly established itself as one of the leading events in the trials calendar. The Bristol lads had, too, a particular flair for finding still further really good, new hills in an already overworked district such as the Cotswolds. Hodgecombe, Middle Drag, Narkover, Tramp's Paradise (Tin Pan Alley) are all attributable to the Bristol Club.

Later on, when the Midland Centre of the M.G. Car Club put on an " open-by-invitation " trial, I had a hand in trials organization myself, so that I speak with feeling when I say it is no mug's game.

After the " Land's End " came the Liverpool Motor Club's " Jeans Gold Cup Trial," around the Buxton area hills. Hollins-clough, Cow Low, Washgates, and Cheeks were all included as non-stop hills in the route, so that, for the most part, it was a case of bouncing from rock to rock, hoping that none of the rocks would penetrate the oil sump, though unhappy incidents of this sort were no uncommon thing among the Derbyshire crags. The Derbyshire scenery as a whole has a certain rugged charm, and many leading trials were regularly held in the Buxton area, but there is no escaping the fact that hills of the Cheeks and Hollinsclough type, and Blackermill also, were terribly hard on the cars, yet presented few difficulties apart from their roughness.

The same area was chosen by Sunbac for their Inter-Club Team Trial a couple of weeks later, but at least they missed out Cheeks and Hollinsclough. Norman Terry, Godfrey Imhof, and myself were entered by Sunbac themselves, as their " B " team. Proceedings opened, as was now customary, with the relay driving-test, the team as a whole being timed, and not the individual drivers. This was as far as Sunbac " B " team got, Imhof demonstrating, in unmistakable fashion, that the rear-axle assembly of the series " T " M.G. was breakable after all. As this was a trial for teams and only team performances counted, there seemed no particular object in Terry and myself continuing, and we cut across to Cow Low, to become spectators.

We were joined by W. J. Green. He told me that he had bought a second car, a " Cracker "-ized series " T " M.G., and was in process of running it in. He had come up from Bedford to Buxton both to spectate on the team trial and to build up some mileage on the new car.

There were some new cars competing also. There were two teams of a new type, 1½-litre Singer, Barnes, Langley (A. H.), and Boughton forming the one, and D. E. Harris, W. C. Butler, and E. B. Booth the second team. The new cars were a good deal different in appearance to their predecessors, having a lot more body space, and the engines were of four cylinders instead of six.

Allard had now got independent suspension for the front wheels of the Special. The manner in which they flapped about on the rocks and boulders of Cow Low was an alarming sight. One was quite prepared to see them part company altogether.

When it was finally all over we learned that it was a mixed team, representing the Lancs and Cheshire Club, that had won the day—J. F. A. Clough (1½-litre Riley), C. E. Stothert (Ballila Fiat), and H. Bolton, formerly of the " Cloggers " Le Mans Singer team (S.S. Jaguar " 100 ").

The " Abingdon," which fell on May 1st, had always been rather a straightforward trial, at any rate so far as the hills were concerned, though not necessarily any the less enjoyable for that, but in 1937 the " Abingdon " reached a new level. The start was moved to " The Prince of Wales," Berkley Road, which is on the main Gloucester–Bristol road. The first hill was almost within sight of the start. It had been scheduled, originally, for the previous November's Fedden Trial, of the Bristol Club, under the name of Tramp's Paradise, but was not actually used, and now had its first introduction into trials in the " Abingdon," rechristened Tin Pan Alley. The approach was (and I say *was*, because it has been altered since) over a grass verge, directly off a main road (secondary, to be strictly accurate). It was a most exciting business, the whole car leaping high in the air, just like a steeplechaser rising to a fence, and swerving alarmingly as it came to earth again in liquid mud. There were ruts reputed to be as much as two feet deep in the track, although, to me, the whole thing appeared to be just an entirely bottomless pit of slime. But the leap in from the main road was great fun.

It was almost impossible to control the steering in the mud, to try to avoid the ruts, but there was a handful of heroes who managed it, all three of the " Musketeer " drivers, Green, trying out the new series " T " M.G., Alf Langley with one of the new Singers, T. C. Wise in the big Ford, and Jack Twyford, from the North-Western Centre of the M.G. Car Club, with a blown " PB."

After that excitement there might well have been a lot of anti-climax. Certainly Axe, Old Hollow, and even Hodgecombe were innocuous, but Sandford and Ashmeads enlivened the proceedings all right. On the lower part of Sandford there was plenty of mud again, but higher up the surface hardened and there was a timed climb, taken on the run, instead of from the usual standing-start, with a nice right-hand corner and a high bank on the inside, making it difficult to judge accurately the sharpness of the corner. I liked Sandford, yet I do not remember it figuring again in any Cotswolds trials in which I competed. Ashmeads, too, had great possibilities, and, indeed, in an event of the Bristol Club earlier in the year, when it had been very wet, it had been a real " stopper." The take-off was still sticky and, as cars went away from the line, the spinning rear wheels shot clods of mud and clay backwards over other competitors following up and awaiting their turn, almost like spraying them with machine-gun bullets.

Just above the starting-line Mr. Kimber crouched in the hedge with his camera. He sent me a photograph of the scene. The car behind mine has the windscreen folded flat over the scuttle, and driver and passenger have their arms up in front of their faces warding off the flying lumps of clay and mud, and the starter and his assistant are crouching with their backs turned. Incidentally, I am pulling a dreadful face, with my tongue stuck out as usual. Ashmeads was good fun, one of the places I am going to look up again when the opportunity presents.

Direction was then taken for Abingdon, but *en route* we turned into Witney aerodrome, for a couple of involved driving tests, first accelerating and reversing round a triangle and then the popular " figure-of-eight." Although a little hard on the transmission, these manœuvres were always great fun, and the more so if opportunity presented, after one's own run, to watch the other fellow.

All in all, therefore, the 1937 " Abingdon " reached a new
" high," and when it was all over, " Dickie " (a boyhood nick-
name from which he never escaped) Green and Jack Bastock
shared the honours, followed closely by Twyford, Wise, and
H. L. Hadley, on the " Grasshopper," supercharged Austin Seven.

As I said at the very beginning of this story, I never " fell "
for the " Edinburgh," so that when I received a set of " regs."
from the Plymouth Motor Club, for an event on Whit-Monday,
I quickly decided to pass up the " Edinburgh " and have a
week-end by the sea, and it so happened that I had never visited
Plymouth.

It was an unfortunate choice. On a hill between Tavistock
and Gunnislake the M.G.'s oil-sump hit a rock and split open.
Once again, having dealt me the fateful blow, thereafter fate
then seemed to repent and play my way. At Horrabridge,
which is on the main Plymouth–Tavistock road, just north of
Yelverton, two sportsmen named Empson and Slade run a
service garage. Slade was competing in the trial on his Le Mans
Singer Nine ; Empson was holding the fort. He came out and
towed me in, got the sump off, and decided to try and weld up
the damage, even if only as a temporary measure to get me on
the road again.

Meanwhile he lent me a car and directed me to one of the
trial's hills, to keep me occupied while he tried to put things
right. But when I got back to his garage, an hour or so later,
he had to admit that the damage was too extensive. On the
Tuesday morning we 'phoned Abingdon for a new sump to be
dispatched. I spent a cheerless day meeting the trains in. As
evening drew on, the sump had still not arrived. I 'phoned
Abingdon again. Consternation ! Stores had packed the sump,
but dispatch had not got it away to the station. I had booked
out from my hotel. On Empson's recommendation I fixed
another one for a night.

The next morning Empson 'phoned me to say that the sump
had arrived at last by the early train, and that he was already
at work fitting it. By the time that I got out to his garage the
car was ready for the road again.

On Saturday, May 29th, Summer and the " Lawrence "
arrived together. What a day ! " Mediterranean " blue sky, without a fleck of cloud, blazing sunshine, shirt sleeves, and open-neck
shirts.

There was an interesting bunch of cars at the start, at Virginia Water. Dickie Green had brought the blown " PB " again, instead of the series " T " on which he had won the " Abingdon." He and I were running on consecutive numbers, eight and nine. John Haesendonck had entered, with JB 7524 of the 1936 " Cream Cracker " M.G.s, and also Reg Andrews, with the one-time Le Mans Midget, with which he had taken a cup in the " Colmore."

There were a number of the H.R.G.s, which were showing themselves admirably suited to trials conditions. Erstwhile and consistently successful Singer driver M. H. Lawson had got one entered. Another was in the hands of W. P. Uglow, whom I had met and got to know during the Plymouth debacle. Another was being driven by E. K. Farley, with whom I remembered having a long chat during the " Coventry," at which time he had been doing his stuff with a rather battered looking four-seater Le Mans Singer. Allard was there, of course. The big engined, light-weight Special was just the thing for the " Lawrence " hills.

I found Philip Flower, with his brother Lionel, stripping the windscreen off the old J2 Midget, which had started life in J. E. S. Jones's hands. Flower told me that he had cut down the weight of the J2 by as much as a hundredweight and a half. A new bonnet had been fitted, with the top panel of thin-gauge aluminium and sides of canvas. Even the already very skimpy mudguards normally standardised on the J2's had been removed and their place taken by the sketchiest possible strips of very light-gauge aluminium. The headlamps and their brackets had been removed and Flower relied upon a single Lucas passlight, set low down on the near side, for driving after dark. The seats and upholstery had been scrapped, and Flower, whom you will remember was without the use of his legs, sat at the wheel in a special light invalid-chair.

Weight-reduction was very much in the air. Fitt had little light mudguards all round his B.M.W., but the prize went to Ken Hutchison. One was accustomed to seeing Hutchison doing his stuff in big Ford coupés and saloons, and sometimes in a Bugatti at Donington, but he turned up for the " Lawrence " in a Ford V8, cut down and skimpily bodied, very much like the Allard in appearance, but seeming even more sketchy.

The weather set the mood for the whole event, so that it was a happy trial, one of the most enjoyable I remember. One worried a bit, at first, over the continuous clicking of the S.U. electric petrol-pump, usually a sign of impending trouble, but the malady seemed to be general, and I had a vague memory that the S.U. concern had said that such a thing might be experienced on the one or, occasionally, two days in the year when real summer visited these isles, and was a harmless phenomenon. Even so Green and I both reckoned we suffered petrol starvation on Tunnel 2, yet, on the other hand, everyone else failed there, except Allard.

On hill after hill Green and myself fought out our private, friendly feud, Dickie, as ever, just those few fifths faster in each of the timed tests, and in that way we came to the final hill, notorious Section Four.

Green went first. The blown " PB " shot away, the bonnet tilted to the skies, sand and shale shot back from the spinning rear wheels. I watched anxiously. The little green car hesitated on the crest, wheels churning ever more furiously, sand and shale flinging out as though from a minor explosion, and all in a second the car came to rest, at the same moment sinking deeply into the loose surface, so that it had to be put into reverse and the engine revved up to get it out again.

Green cleared from the hill and I was given the signal to make my attempt. The ex-" Cracker " put its very best foot (!) forward, bucketed over the sandy ridges in the short take-off to the foot of the hill, rose to the sudden, steep gradient and, almost before one could think, it was all over, the car was away and over the top of the hill, a glorious and exciting moment.

Climbing Section Four entitled me to take a crack at Red Roads, and the " PB " climbed that too. As I came down from the climb of Red Roads, Allard was in position to attack Section Four. Quite what happened I do not know, but to everyone's surprise, the Allard suddenly churned to a standstill on the first part of Section Four, although it had conquered the more difficult Tunnel 2.

Back at Virginia Water, John Haesendonck and Reg Andrews joined Green and myself at the tea-table, and we talked it over. John reckoned that I must have won ; it rather looked that way to me ; most people had undoubtedly failed on two hills at least, but we did not yet know how Hutchison had got along with the spidery Ford. The results proved that John's assumption was correct and this is how they read :

Lawrence Cup.—C. A. N. May (M.G.).

Runner-up.—W. J. Green (M.G.).

Ripley Trophy.—K. Hutchison (Ford V8).

Runner-up.—C. G. Fitt (Frazer-Nash-B.M.W.).

First-Class Award.—S. H. Allard (Allard Special).

Second-Class Awards.—S. L. Chappell (Ford V8) ; M. H. Lawson (H.R.G.) ; S. Curry (Ford V8).

Third-Class Awards.—W. P. Uglow (H.R.G.) ; T. W. Dargue (Frazer-Nash-B.M.W.) ; W. C. N. Norton (Ford V8) ; R. M. Andrews (M.G.) ; E. J. Haesendonck (M.G.) ; G. H. C. Goodban (1½-litre Singer) ; R. A. Macdermid (M.G.) ; A. B. Langley (M.G.) ; J. A. Bastock (M.G.) ; D. E. Harris (M.G.) ; C. J. Turner (1½-litre Singer) ; P. S. Flower (M.G.) ; E. H. Goodenough (M.G.) ; E. H. Jacob (S.S.).

Arising out of the " Lawrence " results there was an amusing little incident which led to a deal of cheery, good-natured leg-pulling, which has been long remembered. *The Motor* gave over a complete page of its photogravure inset to some unusually good photos of cars in action on the " Lawrence " hills. In the left-hand top corner was a three-quarter rear view of Green's car at the exact moment of failure on Section Four. I have the page before me. The M.G.'s spinning rear wheels are digging deeply into the loose surface, and driver and passenger are glancing anxiously backwards over their right shoulders. The caption to the picture reads : " Bang goes the Lawrence Cup. W. J. Green (M.G. Midget), after a fine run, falls a victim to the loose surface and steep gradient of Section Four."

Green, as described, had been sitting pretty for the Cup, by reason of his better times in the special tests, and his failure on this hill was unexpected. " Bang goes the Lawrence Cup " was tagged on to Dickie for a long time, and formed the basis of many a light-hearted leg-pull.

There was no pause. On the following Friday morning more than two hundred cars were off on the Blackpool Rally.

I had a last-minute scramble for a passenger. The course of true love had temporarily ceased to run smoothly. The lady who should have sat on my left decided to stay at home instead. Then I had a sudden idea. I looked through the programme and found that one or two prominent names were missing.

Desperate, I rang up Norman Terry. No, there was no special reason why he had not entered ; he had no other fixture for the week-end ; he just hadn't thought about a rally. Well, of course, if I was really stuck. . . . I was really stuck, so Norman went to Blackpool after all, *and* enjoyed it.

It were a " reet champion do." Birmingham starters went up to Chester, and then on to Higher Hodder, which is north-east of Preston. Here there was a section common to all routes, wherein was staged a stop-and-go test on a deceptively steep bank known as Birdie Brow. There followed some secondary road stuff which had to be covered exactly to a set speed. Thereafter the route went on up to The Lakes, before doubling back to Blackpool.

On Saturday morning, under threatening skies, the two special tests were run off on the lower promenade at Blackpool. As ever, some drivers were brilliant and breath-taking, some were unfortunate and either hit things or broke " bits " (sometimes both), some were comical, some, like myself, were just slow. In more than five years of competition work I do not think there were more than a couple of times when I managed to get through a set of these tests just that bit faster than the next man, and it was not for want of trying.

Some folk seem to have a flair for this sort of thing, a combination of superfine judgment and dead accurate " placing." In this connection one immediately thinks of the cool mathematically precise efforts of Alf Langley, the determined performances by Dickie Green, the rip-snorting, but always very fast runs of Godfrey Imhof, and the remarkable large-car efforts of T. C. Wise.

They were all at Blackpool. I remember Wise was electrifying with the open-bodied V8 Ford. He actually made fastest combined times in the two tests, but he had defaulted somewhere *en route*, and the Rally winner proved to be a new star, J. F. A. Clough, with one of the sleek, two-seater, 1½-litre Rileys. Green, airing the series " T " again, won the 10 h.p. Open Car Class. Imhof actually returned fastest times for the tests in this class, but, like Wise, had defaulted on the road section. Alf Langley was runner-up to Clough.

Thereafter it rained, but, even so, some good fun was had down at the South Shore Pleasure Beach. John Haesendonck, Green, and myself were photographed, all three on a single

" property " motor-cycle, Green wearing an awful white helmet.
I remember Alf Langley exhorting his crew to super-efforts (not
that, in fact, they could really influence the decision) in one of
the cars on the Great Racer. Some of the boys were most anxious
to go through the evolutions of the special tests all over again on
the Bumper Cars. Aye, it were a " reet champion do."

Soon afterwards I took the car back to Abingdon for a complete overhaul, the oil-consumption having reached astronomical
figures. I was not going to want it for nearly three weeks, as
Frank Kemp (M.G. Car Club Midland Centre secretary) and
his wife and myself were off for a cruise, having arranged to
entrust our health and happiness to the tender mercies of the
Peninsular and Oriental Steam Navigation Company for a
fortnight. In consequence we were in Naples while Macdermid
was winning the " Brighton–Beer."

CHAPTER VIII

" Non-Stop " Continues

I EXPECT it was purely imagination, but, somehow, the ex-" Cracker " never seemed *quite* the same again after I got it back with the new engine in. Certainly, I did not have *quite* as much success with it thereafter.

Its first outing, after the running-in period had been completed, was in a trial in Wales, an event of the Oxton Motor Club, with the start at Llangollen.

Green was there, of course ; Dickie hardly ever missed an event. Norman Terry was present, and so was Hutchison, with the fierce Ford. A fresh coterie of motor-sport enthusiasts had come into being, and had formed a new club in the Midlands. They called it the Hagley and District Light Car Club, and two of its leading members, both of whom I had met and got to know in various events, were at Llangollen. They were A. R. Kendrick (blown " PB ") and Norman Grove (modified, trials-equipped, series " T " M.G.).

Kendrick returned the best performance of the day, and from about this period on I saw a good deal of him. He won an M.C.C. Triple Award in the 1938 season. Green was runner-up in this event, with Hutchison " best over 10 h.p." Grove, who later joined the M.G. Car Club Midland Centre committee, and will be met again in this book, was one of the first-class award winners, the old ex-" Cracker " managing one also.

The following week-end brought the Motor-Cycling Club's Torquay Rally. What I had to say about the special tests at Blackpool applied equally at Torquay, although Green was off form for once, and it was " the Colonel " (J. Maurice Toulmin) who made best performance in the hotly contested 10 h.p. Open Car Class. Best performance of the day was returned by Leslie Johnson, on the ex-Miss Goodban Frazer-Nash-B.M.W., fast becoming a new " menace."

Geoffrey Boughton was close behind him with the new $1\frac{1}{2}$-litre Singer, while, at the other end of the scale, John Haesendonck stripped the crown-wheel on JB 7524, and Imhof was unluckiest of all. His car ran away downhill, while he was not in it, of course, and was damaged against a wall. The weather was magnificent, rivalling the " Lawrence " week-end.

It was after Torquay that I first really got to know E. H. (Eddy) Goodenough and proceeded to build up another close and lasting friendship. Eddy was a dyed-in-the-wool M.G. enthusiast, and the blue, Marshall supercharged, " PB " M.G., AHT 1 was a familiar sight at all the leading events, but somehow we had never sort of got together before.

One way and another we must have had quite a summer in 1937. After the sunshine of the " Abingdon," the " Lawrence," and the Torquay Rally, there came a brilliant August Bank Holiday week-end, so that the " Barnstaple " was more of a holiday " conducted tour " than ever.

It used to be fashionable, about this period, to deplore the fact that all adventure had gone out of modern life. Those who spoke in this manner had never, of course, competed in motor trials.

On the Wednesday immediately preceding the " Barnstaple," the M.G.'s radiator sprang a leak, the sort that could not be ignored. I contacted Lloyd-Jones. He was, as I had feared, up to his eyes in it. He put me straight in touch with the firm to whom he usually took his radiator repair jobs. I fled round there. They could manage the actual repair, but it was not a job that could be done with the radiator in position, and they could not release a mechanic to remove the radiator. There was no alternative but to tackle the dismantling myself, and, with the sketchy tool-kit carried on the car, I set to work. Fortune smiled upon me. I got the radiator off without even one of the water hoses sustaining damage, and, very surprised, actually reassembled it, all between breakfast and lunch.

Friday afternoon I started out for Minehead, to be ready for the start from there on the Saturday morning. Beyond Gloucester the clutch suddenly started to slip. I decided to push on to Bristol : the slip was only under load. I turned down White-ladies Road and burst in upon Macdermid. Duly sympathetic, he took me along to " his man." The clutch was investigated, worked upon, and I was asked to try it again. There was a narrow passage between high walls at the side of the garage, and I rushed up and down it, snap-changing, and making " racing " getaways. There was a decided improvement. Further treatment was given, and in due course I continued to Minehead.

Bank Holiday Saturday dawned fine and clear, with a promise of considerable heat, and big crowds were about from a very early hour. I waited anxiously for my passenger, Pat Reynolds, who was starting out the same morning from between Gloucester and Bristol. In a rush and a flurry Macdermid arrived from Bristol, having, he averred, travelled the entire way on the right-hand side of the road, inferring, of course, that the traffic stream was unbroken even at this hour. With five minutes to go, Reynolds arrived, breathless after a dreadful struggle through the traffic congestion.

At the start one noticed the increasing number of H.R.G.s competing, and also the unusual sight of Alf Langley in a Ford V8 coupé. It was a car with a history, having been driven through the Monte Carlo Rally by J. W. Whalley. It was equipped with a four-speed pre-selector gear-box.

By way of Doverhay, Edbrooke, and Tarr Steps—all non-stop hills, from a standing-start, of course—the route led to Wellshead, where was staged the special test, a double stop-and-go test. Eddy Goodenough went away in front of me, and with a heart-rending clatter, the M.G.'s crown-wheel stripped. The little blue car was pushed clear of the fairway, and I arranged to return that way at the conclusion of the trial to see what I could do for Eddy, leaving with him a spare crown-wheel and pinion I happened to have with me. I realized as I went on that it had come out of a J2 type M.G. and would not be of service to him. But it was not wasted. Hardly had I gone on my way than along came a J2 M.G., driven by G. F. Pentony, from London, and promptly stripped its crown-wheel right where Goodenough had become an unwilling spectator.

After the finish of the trial it was found that the formula that was to have been used for the allocation of the awards penalized the larger cars excessively, and altogether the results were a bit shaky. Macdermid was at first declared the winner, but it had not been appreciated, apparently, that Mac had, for some time, been carrying out his slogan, " It's better blown," and a revised set of results gave me the Gliksten Trophy, with Dickie Green as runner-up, though both of us had been seconds slower in the special test than G. H. Robins (H.R.G.).

After lunch, at Barnstaple, I took Reynolds back to Minehead to collect his car, wife, and children, and then set out to find Goodenough. I caught up with the blue M.G., forlorn by the roadside, between Wheddon Cross and Exford. Eddy had managed to contact his father by telephone, and Goodenough senior was coming down from their home at Redhill, on the Bristol–Bridgwater road, with the " family " Riley to tow the M.G. home. He arrived while I was there. He had had a wicked journey in the congested mass of the Bank Holiday traffic. So even " a sun-dried Barnstaple," to quote *The Autocar*, was not without incident, although, of course, I am not suggesting that tearing up back axles is everyone's cup of tea as a form of Bank Holiday recreation.

For most of us it was an all-pleasure week-end. Frank and Mrs. Kemp and myself, after spending the Saturday night at " The Royal and Fortescue " at Barnstaple, went on, on Sunday morning, to Woolacombe, where, rather to our surprise, for after all it was August, we obtained accommodation at the Woolacombe Bay Hotel. Round the corner at Coombe Martin my partner in business, Leonard Simmons, and his wife were holidaying with S. K. Ridley, who was on our M.G. Committee when P. J. Evans Ltd. had the M.G. agency, and his wife and child. As the sun shone continuously, the week-end could hardly have been improved upon from any angle, and it was Wednesday morning before the Kemps and myself started back to Birmingham.

On the immediately following Friday I was heading south again, to Bournemouth this time, for speed trials in Poole Park on the Saturday. Again the sun was shining ; indeed it was particularly hot in the park. I joined forces with John Haesendonck and his wife, and John's brother, Ernest, with his fiancée, for another really enjoyable week-end. Ernest had a blown " PB " M.G. with a special light body, more or less of racing type. It proved faster over the course at Poole than either John Haesendonck's car or my own, and won the 1100 c.c. and 1½-litre super-sports classes. John's car was second, but my own seemed a little off form. We basked in the sun and watched the " racers " (drivers supporting purely speed events) perform. C. E. C. Martin set a new course record with the maroon 1½-litre E.R.A., closely followed by G. R. Hartwell with the ex- E. R. Hall K3 M.G. Magnette, and D. H. C. Fry with the weird-looking, but always very fast, hybrid, the Freikaiserwagen.

The South-Western Centre of the M.G. Car Club provided, on Saturday, August 21st, yet a further excuse for a seaside

week-end, by staging driving tests in the car park adjoining the
rugby football ground at Weston-super-Mare, and again it was
an all-sunshine week-end. I went down to Weston on my
series " T " M.G., and in the company of Frank Kemp and Pat
Reynolds, in Frank's Zoller-blown " N " Magnette.

It was a cheerful, if somewhat dusty and grimy, afternoon.
Most of the entrants were in holiday mood, and I rarely remember
seeing cars flung about with such delightful abandon and with
such an utter lack of regard for consequences. The surface was
mainly of sifted cinders, and cars slid and swerved in clouds of
fine dust, brakes squealed, gear-boxes protested, tyres folded
under. Godfrey Imhof gave the most vigorous performance I
think I have ever witnessed, making the white M.G. do everything but sit up and talk, and although, by all the rules and
regulations, the car should have broken into small pieces, Imhof's
terrific verve was rewarded by his making easily the fastest times.

At the other end of the scale, Kemp had the misfortune to
strip the crown-wheel of the Magnette, in the first of the three
tests. While most of us had arranged to stay the night in Weston
and make a week-end of it, Kemp and Reynolds specially wanted
to be back in Birmingham the same night. The problem was
solved by their returning to Birmingham in my car, after I had
arranged to stay the night and get a lift home on Sunday afternoon with Alf Langley, in the Monte Carlo Ford. I was enabled
to stay the night only after the management at the Royal Pier
Hotel had been persuaded to put a bed up for me in the writing
room.

I have found some pictures I took during the meeting. They
bear out my description of the event as cheerful and care-free,
inasmuch as Macdermid and Crawford appear, in one photograph, to be in the throes of an all-in wrestling match, while in
another Macdermid is performing a " strip-tease " act.

I ran the M.G. in the speed hill-climb at Shelsley Walsh.
Having been a spectator there for years, I had often yearned to
be on the other side of the fence, and I felt that, with the supercharged " PB," I could have a go without disgracing myself as
to the time taken. I ran the car stripped, taking it out to the
hill on a trailer, towed behind my 30-cwt. Bedford covered van,
with Lloyd-Jones's " Triangle Special " Lea-Francis wedged
inside the van. I did not get an opportunity to weigh the car,
but it was surprising what a lot of pieces it proved possible to

remove when you really set about it—mudguards and their supports, all lamps and brackets, windscreen and hood, of course, spare-wheel bracket, front tray and number plates, floor carpeting and part of the upholstery, even the passenger's seat (I was still using my separate bucket-seats).

Towards the end of the practice period, on the Friday afternoon, John Haesendonck arrived to give me moral support. I needed it ; the car was being a bit temperamental, as it could at times, usually in the matter of plugs, being fussy over a thousand in the plug gaps. I had gone *de luxe* with a set of LA 14's (a sparking plug made specially for racing by the Champion Co.), but the recessed points were a bit tricky to adjust. Haesendonck " taxied " me home, stayed overnight at my home, and ran me back to the hill in the morning.

I. was not the only trials driver trying his hand among the racers. L. G. Johnson was there, but driving a special supercharged B.M.W. instead of his usual trials car, and H. L. Hadley was driving one of the single-seater, racing Austins. Some of the speed merchants lifted an eyebrow at our getaways. There is nothing like trials to teach you how to leave line " A " at speed upon receiving a given signal.

The ex-" Cracker " did not give of its best at Shelsley, and the fastest run was in 52 seconds, where I had hoped to get down to 50, but I thoroughly enjoyed the experience, and, if ever the opportunity presents, I shall not hesitate to drive there again. It is odd what a fascination there is about this type of event, bearing in mind that the car is in action only a few seconds at a time, but it is a very real fascination.

Speed was again the keynote of the next event—the Motor Cycling Club's Members' Day Meeting at Brooklands. Here, as was customary, the trials drivers formed the bulk of the entry. The sun had ceased to shine ; in fact it rained quite heavily, so that as a wearer of glasses, without which I cannot see, I was very much at a disadvantage. For the first few laps in the one-hour run, while the cars were still bunched and the air was filled with fine spray, I could hardly see at all, and had to reduce speed until I was of two minds whether to continue, not feeling at all safe. The cars soon spread out, in the odd way that they always do in these one-hour " blinds," and I was able to clear my vision and " get cracking." A few slow laps take a deuce of a lot of fetching back in the space of an hour, and it was at once obvious that my cherished hopes of covering 80 miles in the hour would not be realized. That the ex-" Crackers " were well capable of this was convincingly demonstrated by John Haesendonck, with a fine run of a shade over 84 miles in the hour.

I had a marvellous scrap in one of the short handicap events. I was on the same handicap mark as Fotheringham-Parker, who had had racing experience with Alvis cars, but on this occasion was driving a Ford V8 coupé. We were bonnet to bonnet all the way, first one then the other gaining a fraction of advantage. The M.G.'s revolution counter went right up above 6500 (equivalent to a road speed of about 95 m.p.h.) along the Railway Straight, and in the final run in, I led the Ford by scarcely a bonnet's length.

When I went in to sign the finisher's sheet, at the end of the hour run, and Mrs. Masters (wife of J. A. Masters, the club's secretary) tried to engage me in conversation, I realized that I was almost stone deaf, a condition which did not work off completely until the following morning. As soon as Kerswell, my passenger for the week-end, and myself had put back the windscreen, and generally put the car in trim for the road again, we set off for Taunton. On the morrow was scheduled the West Hants Club's Knott Trophy Trial, starting from Tiverton, and marking the opening of the autumn trials programme.

Overnight the weather changed completely, and the trial took place in blazing sunshine. At the start at Tiverton, on Sunday morning, I was reminded of F. L. M. Harris's words, quoted earlier, in connection with the 1936 Gloucester Trial : " I suggest it is principally the few spectacular figures in the trials game who keep the sport alive and vigorous." Macdermid, Bastock, Arch Langley, J. E. S. Jones, Allard, Warburton, Flower, Johnson, were all at the start, Johnson, like myself, having come on from Brooklands.

There were three non-stop hills which I had not seen before, Lee Cross, Brook, and Pilemoor, the latter far the most difficult of the three, but it was Widlake that pretty well decided the issue. A back tyre went flat on my car within a few yards of starting the climb, but whether I should have got up otherwise I am doubtful, since only five were successful—Johnson, Macdermid, Jones, Allard, and D. P. Kirkman. Kirkman won the Knott Trophy. His " vintage " Alvis, with bolt-on type steel-spoke wheels, had mudguards (!) of plywood, a fore-shortened body, mainly of the same material, with an old-fashioned straight-up, two-piece windscreen, no bonnet, and three spare wheels. Macdermid, Jones, Allard, and myself shared out the other main awards, and Allard, Warburton, and myself collected the team prize, Warburton having persuaded me to join forces with Allard and himself at the start.

Although the Wye Valley Club's annual trial for the Hereford City Trophy had not previously had the support of the leading drivers, many of them turned up, on October 10th, for the 1937 event, perhaps a case of great minds think alike. Certainly I had not known in advance of the event that it was going to enjoy this support, and I am not sure really what had prompted me to enter this particular event myself. I can only suppose that it came on an otherwise blank week-end, and the prospect of exploring new ground was always attractive.

The " Cream Cracker " trio was there and also the " Grass-hopper " Austin team, but with the third car driven, not by H. L. Hadley, but Alfred (Singer) Langley, the Singer team having disbanded.

It was an odd sort of a trial. Most of the hills were taken on the run, instead of from a standing-start, and as weather conditions had left most of the course in a dry condition, the event became largely a series of speed hill-climbs, the results being decided entirely on the times recorded in the several special tests. Had it been wet, there would undoubtedly have been fun and games on Pont-y-Weston, this being the one hill of obvious possibilities—possibilities which were to be realized in later events. It was a longish hill, starting between high hedges, with a rocky surface to start with, but becoming grass surfaced and rutted higher up, where it left the protection of the hedges. There was another hill which rivalled Buxton at its rockiest. Cusop Dingle started out of a water-splash and went up between high banks with a surface of rock outcrop strewn with fearsome boulders, more damaging than difficult.

The " Cream Cracker " boys (Toulmin, Crawford, Jones) won the Hereford City Trophy, and the Zimmerman Cup for best individual performance was gained by F. D. Gilson (Allard Special). I had met Gilson, a Wolverhampton man, a number of times in events in the Midlands, usually driving an M.G. Magna, with which he did not seem to have any particular fortune. The Allard he had purchased was not, at any rate in external appearance, an exact replica of Allard's own car. It was much less " home built," having a neat four-seater body, of quite smart appearance, more adequate mudguarding than Allard's own car, and generally a more professional finish throughout.

Let me introduce another new name into this story. My passenger on this trial was A. E. (Jim) Frost. I had known Frost for quite a while, usually meeting him in the rôle of passenger to Jack Bastock. Frost did not, however, intend to be permanently a passenger (in any sense of the word) and was preparing to join the ranks of the regular drivers with a Frazer-Nash-B.M.W.

For a description of the Motor-Cycling Club's One-Day Sporting Trial, in the Buxton district, on October 23rd, I take the liberty of reproducing part of an article by R. A. Macdermid (*The Sports Car*, December 1937) : " Rain, rain, rain : pitiless and unceasing from leaden skies ; coursing in little rivulets between hoods and screens and serving but to emphasize that the weather protection of the average car in trials trim, whilst perhaps superior to that of a bicycle, still falls short of a good umbrella. Yes, rain was the keynote of the M.C.C. sporting trial at Buxton, and the relative easiness of the course showed how a steady downpour washes hills clean of spin-provoking slime."

The event could hardly have been summed up more accurately or more pithily. There were few of us who did not have to dry out articles of clothing after the trial, so that I did not envy Eddy Goodenough and his sister, who had arranged to drive straight back to Bristol instead of staying the night at Buxton like the majority of us.

The " One-Day Sporting " constituted the final round for the 1937 M.C.C. Team Championship (decided on the cumulative performances of the teams competing in all of the club's road trials within a twelve-months' period, *i.e.* " Land's End," " Edinburgh," " Exeter," " Torquay," and " One-Day Sporting "). The winners were the " Cream Cracker " trio—Toulmin, Crawford, and Jones.

The " Experts " came up next on the calendar. I still had vivid memories of my ride with Crawford in the 1936 version of this rough, tough event, and I prevailed upon the invaluable

" Fido " Kerswell to be my passenger. I also had the differential lock put back in the rear-axle assembly.

Dickie Green, John Haesendonck, and myself had teamed together for this event, Green's car being almost identical with the 1936 " Cream Cracker " cars of John's and mine. There was a new hill, but, for once in a way, no advance rumours had come out concerning it, and the name Colly indicated nothing.

I feel sure that I am right in saying that Colly has been used only twice, in the Experts Trials of 1937 and 1938, and only seven competitors tackled it in the 1937 event. Colly starts as little more than a V-bottomed ditch, between very high banks, with foliage meeting overhead and giving a tunnel effect. It emerges into the light of day at a right-handed, right-angle corner, at which point the gradient stiffens sharply, and there are some fierce rock steps. As it continues, still between hedges and very narrow, there is mud, ruts, rock outcrop, and ledges like a flight of stairs. It is the ditch at the beginning that is the most alarming part. The shelving sides go down to meet in a sharp, deep V, so that cars have to be forced to straddle the ditch— a precarious performance.

This hill is marked clearly on a 1-inch scale Ordnance Survey map (sheet 119—Exmoor), and is just outside the little village of Luxborough, which, in its turn, is about four miles almost due south of Dunster. If you leave Luxborough church on your right hand and face westwards, the approach to Colly is the next turning to the left. The track at first goes downhill from the main lane, passes through a water-splash, and then Colly proper is the track going off to the left, just above the cottage. It is worth the while of anyone who finds himself in the neighbourhood to have a look at the toughest thing ever put before the trials fraternity. Mere words cannot convey an adequate description of the horror that is Colly.

I did not witness the accident to Allard which caused the abandonment of the hill in the 1937 event. Six competitors tackled the hill ahead of Allard, of whom Macdermid and Hutchison were actually successful. As I waited back in the main lane by my car, I heard, faintly, what sounded uncommonly like a crash and the Allard's exhaust note cut short at the same time. In a matter of seconds the word flashed back down the line of waiting cars that Allard had overturned. We ran along the track towards the scene of the accident. As I came up from the water-splash, Allard and his wife came round the corner from off the hill. Both were well smeared in blood and looked very shaken up and uncertain.

The car was upside down, bridging the V-bottom of the ditch. It was quite evident that Allard had been unable to keep the car straddling the V, and when the two wheels on one side of the car dropped into the cleft, that was sufficient, at the speed at which Allard was travelling, to cause the car to over-turn.

I then learned that the car was not actually Allard's property any longer : he had sold it to Warburton shortly before the trial, but, not having any suitable alternative car on which to compete in the " Experts," there had been a mutual agreement between the two drivers for Allard to use the car in this event, and for it to pass into Warburton's possession immediately afterwards. Warburton told me, later, what a struggle they had to get the car out from the narrow confines of Colly, it being impossible to put it back on its wheels at the point where it had capsized.

Somewhat chastened, competitors were by-passed to the summit of Colly, and continued to Widlake. For the first time I climbed Widlake non-stop, a grand thrill, so that I remember well that Fido and I sang lustily at the tops of our voices as the old " Cracker " slid into the farmyard at Widlake's summit for the very first time.

Triumph was short lived : the car failed on the first corner of Cloutsham—punishment, no doubt, for over-confidence, since I had secretly prided myself that Cloutsham, though difficult, was a hill which I had got weighed up. Green had failed on Cloutsham, just in front of me, and had suffered damage to the M.G.'s front oil-pipe. I was carrying a spare, so we stopped and changed it.

After Downscombe, again rough rather than difficult, we went out on to the moor for Cowcastle and Picked Stones. No river larks this year, though, Cowcastle being approached from a different direction—and what an approach ! The track dis-appeared completely at times, so that flags had been stuck in the ground by the organizers to indicate the direction to be followed ! Cowcastle proved to be a really good hill, with one particularly sticky right-hand corner on grass, where I had a very anxious moment. I took a gamble on snapping the gear-lever through to second, and it worked, spin checking moment-arily as the higher gear went home, and the car being kept in motion.

By the time we got down to Picked Stones, Haesendonck's car had lost the entire silencing system. Green and myself both stuck on the left-hand hairpin above the splash. There was quite a bit of fun there actually. J. E. S. Jones, approaching too widely, got the M.G.'s offside wheels over the edge and the car had to be hauled back with a horse. Warburton's big Vauxhall had to be manhandled round too. Yet L. G. Johnson took the B.M.W. round without a reverse, a most incredible performance.

After all that excitement Mannacott tunnel was very straight-forward, and from there it was but a short run to Blackmoor Gate—and something to eat.

One of the timed tests did not take place and, as a result, there were two ties in the results list :

Best Performance.—J. M. Toulmin and A. G. Imhof (M.G.s).

Runners-up.—K. Hutchison (Ford V8) and C. D. Buckley (Austin).

Ballards Trophy (best club team).—The " Cream Crackers " (Toulmin, Crawford, Jones).

Mellano Trophy (best one-make team).—C. A. N. May, W. J. Green, E. J. Haesendonck (M.G.s).

For the Vesey Cup Trial, on November 6th, Sunbac used substantially the same course as that which had been em-ployed by the Wye Valley Club for their Hereford City Trophy Trial, even to the inclusion of boulder-strewn Cusop Dingle.

Personally I have always felt that this type of obstacle has little to recommend it. On the average the Cusop Dingles cause only a very small percentage of outright failures (four in the " Vesey "), but the sum-total of damage sustained by competing cars, could it be calculated and tabulated, would represent a substantial figure. In most cases such damage would be more or less of a superficial nature, but there would always be at least one poor unfortunate who would sustain major damage. Cusop's victim in the " Vesey " was my old friend Kenneth Delingpole. Delingpole had parted with the white Singer and

acquired a supercharged " PB " M.G., and after going to considerable pains to put the little car into full trials trim, was giving
it its first outing. One of Cusop's boulders went through the
M.G.'s oil-sump and the car went home on the end of a tow-
rope.

In sharp contrast to. the Dingle, Pont-y-Weston, particularly
when wet, was the sort of hill that was always good fun to have a
crack at, and, except when bone dry, usually productive of a
bigger crop of failures (thirteen, in the " Vesey," as against four
at Cusop). *The Autocar* (November 12th, 1937) summed up the
position at Pont-y-Weston in a manner on which I cannot
improve :

" First of the hills proper was Pont-y-Weston, a longish
gradient between hedges, more formidable by reason of mud
than sheer steepness. Most competitors changed up early to
second, and, if they had enough engine-power to keep the wheels
spinning, ' made the grade ' in a series of slides and a rearward
spouting fountain of earth clods. If, on the other hand, they
had to change down again, the loss of way frequently resulted
in failure on the upper reaches."

The report went on to say : " . . . But among the good
climbs were those of May's M.G., which shot up, the passenger
waving cheerfully, in a veritable explosion of mud." This being
a Sunbac event, the invaluable Fido was busy on the organizing
side, and I had as passenger the cheery and enthusiastic Mrs.
Alfred Langley, who, if my memory serves me rightly, was waving
to her own husband.

Towards the end of the trial came a cleverly sited, timed
driving test, the artificial garages being positioned with great
cunning, leaving little or no room for manœuvre if the car was
not placed correctly at each change of direction. I was not the
only one to come adrift there. On the other hand, the way the
thing could be handled was demonstrated to such purpose by
Dickie Green that his performance here, combined, of course,
with non-stop climbs of all the hills, won for him the Vesey Cup
for best performance of the day. Only two-fifths of a second
slower, J. F. A. Clough, Blackpool Rally winner, took the Carless
Cup for best performance over 1100 c.c., and to C. D. Buckley
with the " Grasshopper " Austin went the Watson Gwynne
Bowl for best performance under 1100 c.c. Clough was also in
the winning team, of which the other two members were

Norman Terry and T. C. Wise ; runners-up Green, Jim Frost, and myself.

It was a nice little trial, but the full possibilities of the Herefordshire area were yet to be developed, and it was Sunbac who were to exploit them, in their 1938 inter-team trial, but that will come up in its proper place.

As was their wont, the Bristol Club dug up three new non-stop hills for their Fedden Trial the following week-end—Narkover, Tor, and Cow Kilcott. Hodgecombe, Nailsworth, and Old Hollow also figured on the route-card, so that had it been wet this route would have been very severe. But with one or two vivid exceptions, such as the " One-Day Sporting," the autumn had been a dry one, with high winds to dry the surfaces of the hills still further.

I had one of those days which, I suppose, all of us experience now and again, when I could do nothing right at all, so that to me all of the hills seemed very difficult, Narkover in particular, although in fact only four failures were recorded there. Narkover, which is not a map name and of whose exact locality I am a bit hazy, nevertheless had possibilities, and these were subsequently realized in the 1938 " Fedden."

Cow Kilcott proved to be the most difficult of the three new hills, and, just to show the perversity of things, this was about the only hill on which I managed a non-stop climb that day. Cow Kilcott is mostly grass, and quite steep, with a sharp left-hand corner. It would have been a " stopper " of the first order when really wet, and yet I do not recollect its being used again.

But the *pièce de résistance* of the 1937 " Fedden " was our old friend Old Hollow, which was every bit as difficult as it had been when it nearly wrecked the 1935 " Gloucester," the occasion of its first introduction into trials. Curiously, Old Hollow had been strangely ineffective since that first time, but for the " Fedden " it was right back on form. Admittedly the re-start line was placed a good deal higher than it had been in the 1935 " Gloucester," but, on the other hand, there had not been heavy rain all the preceding night on the occasion of the " Fedden."

I had an early number, and after I had failed there I parked my car beyond the top of the hill and walked back to watch the efforts of later competitors. Car after car was unable to leave the line, wheels spun, engines raced, smoke came off the wildly churning tyres, but to no avail. Then along came Philip Flower with the veteran J2. The flag fell, Flower eased off the big outside handle which combines clutch and brake on his car (you remember, of course, that he had not the use of his legs), the M.G. motored quietly off the line, and wuffled away effortlessly round the corner, a most incredible performance. I saw Dennis Buckley also make a splendid get-away and climb nonstop, and a terrific performance by Macdermid. It was almost a case of an irresistible force (the supercharged engine of the " Musketeer " M.G.) meeting an immovable body (the re-start area on Old Hollow). The M.G. seemed to sit literally for seconds in a haze of smoke until sheer force alone appeared to triumph, and the red car shot away. I think that even the organizers were surprised at the effectiveness of Old Hollow, and it was primarily on the performances here that was decided the winners of the unusually large number of cups and trophies offered for competition in the " Fedden." :

Roy Fedden Trophy.—C. D. Buckley (747 c.c. Austin s/c).
Daphne Trophy (Runner-up).—P. S. Flower (847 c.c. M.G.).
Committee Cup (third best).—K. N. Hutchison (Ford V8).
Duckham Cup (fourth best).—W. J. Green (939 c.c. M.G. s/c).

It seems that I missed a good thing by not going on the Torbay and Totnes Club's English Riviera Trial. Actually there were two open-by-invitation events that week-end, the other being the Harrow Car Club's Cottingham Memorial Trophy Trial in the Chilterns, and I do not think that anyone managed to compete in both trials. I happened to pick the Harrow Club's event.

To the English Riviera Trial went, among others, the " Musketeer " M.G.s (Macdermid, Langley, and Bastock), the " Grasshopper " Austins (Buckley, Scriven, and Alf Langley), and Dickie Green. There were, apparently, two really difficult hills, Snail's Castle and the inelegantly named S.o.B. To my considerable regret I have never seen either of these two hills, which were much talked about by those who competed in this trial. I must, therefore, refer you to Macdermid's descriptions of these two sections (*The Sports Car*, January 1938) :

" . . . The former (S.o.B.) is not unlike Widlake, though steeper, where the driver can approach at speed and then with the throttle wide open must leave everything else to the car. No one gained a view of the summit, and of its type I think S.o.B. is as difficult a hill as any I know. Snail's Castle, on the other hand, could be climbed by the average trials car quite easily, but only if adequately handled, and its difficulty lies in a series of very quick hairpins. . . ."

Even so, it was but a select band that coped successfully with Snail's Castle, the " Musketeers," the " Grasshoppers," Green and Imhof. There was another horror, rejoicing in the name of Autobahn, which, although not claiming quite so many failures, was as tough almost as Colly, comprising ruts of unfathomable depth and great slabs of stone. In fact, I gathered that all in all the English Riviera Trial ran a close second to the " Experts " for being rough, tough, and enjoyable.

Dennis Buckley scored his second win in successive week-ends ; Hadley, runner-up ; Langley (Alfred), best visitor ; and the " Grasshoppers " taking the team award—in fact, almost an Austin " grand slam," broken only by Macdermid, best member, and D. Loader (Ford V8), best saloon perform-ance.

The " Cottingham," by contrast, was fairly straightforward, only one hill giving any real trouble. This was a grass slope in a field, right at the start, the surface frost-bound. It was christened, appropriately enough, Spinning Wheel. Quite re-markable things happened here, some people hardly attaining any forward motion at all, others, often with apparently less suitable cars, just motored up without fuss. I think the secret lay almost entirely in the get-away : once spin was started it was almost impossible to control on the frosty grass. I took off with vastly more restraint than was my custom, and then just toured up quietly without any trouble.

Unfortunately I did not exercise the same restraint at the downhill brake test, and promptly forfeited all chance of an award.

As the early morning frost thawed out under the influence of the late autumn sunshine, which shone down from cloudless blue skies, the rest of the non-stop hills, Tunnel Slide, Jacob's Ladder, Mounts's Hill, Rutty Lane, and Hale Acre Farm were mostly mud-larking, particularly Hale Acre.

Despite two timed special tests being staged, there was a tie for the Cottingham Trophy, between T. Bushell-King (Frazer-Nash) and C. W. Taylor (1½-litre Singer). Philip Flower won the Visitor's Cup.

I went, for the second year in succession, to the Kentish Border Car Club's November Trial, in Kent. As in the previous year, it proved to be a most enjoyable event. Although the sun shone strongly all day, the hills were far from dry and only four of us got round without fault—Dickie Green (inevitably), Allard (of course), W. C. N. Norton, and myself. Green was driving the blown " PB." Allard was using the car he had built for Gilson, AUK 795, and with which, it seemed, that driver was not quite happy, so that Allard was trying the car himself under actual trials conditions. Norton was driving a V8 cabriolet, said to be of 1933 vintage, and painted bright yellow and black, and having sawn-off mudguards. Three such cars were competing under the team name of " The Jabberwocks," the other two drivers being D. Loader and H. Koppenhagen.

Within two miles of the start was by far the most difficult hill of the trial, Knatt's Valley, alias La Grimpe. Knatt's Valley proved to be very much on the lines of Rushmere, though not quite as steep, and with the actual track rather more clearly defined, but grass-surfaced the same as Rushmere. This is the sort of hill where, as a rule, the car is of more importance than the driver. Sufficient speed must be attained in the short take-off to carry over the steep pitch of the hill proper, supercharged and big-engined cars naturally standing the best chance of achieving this. The take-off at Knatt's Valley, that particular day, was decidedly sticky, and too fierce an attempt to build up speed before hitting the hill proper resulted in wheelspin and *not* road speed. Undoubtedly the take-off got worse, due to the fact that, at first, the ground was hardened slightly by over-night frost, but this thawed out under a strong winter sun very soon.

The eleven who climbed Knatt's (more than seventy started) were all in the first half of the entry, but even so, I was a little surprised to find out later that my ascent was the last non-stop climb recorded, and that after I had gone there were thirty-six failures in a row.

The two other " problem pieces " were Shrubbs Wood

hairpin and Stowting, though that is not to suggest that all the other hills were just " fill-ins." There were eleven hills altogether, and while there was some straightforward stuff, Palmstead, Watsole Street, and Limeworks, there were a good few copy-books blotted at Switchback and Buckwell Bank, both of which were new to me, and good fun.

Shrubbs Wood, in contrast to Knatt's, is a " driver's hill," consisting of a hairpin corner of which the apex of the corner is the lowest point, so that, from either direction, there is a down-hill approach, immediately followed, after the negotiation of the actual hairpin of course, by an uphill pull-away. The surface being mainly earth and leaf mould, it is a tricky proposition. The corner has to be approached sufficiently slowly to avoid a front-wheel slide into the hedge when the steering is locked over for the turn, yet sufficient " way " must be maintained to " carry over " the sticky little climb which immediately follows, any sudden acceleration on coming out of the corner resulting in wild wheelspin.

Stowting used to have quite a reputation, and probably I have not seen it at its worst, but, anyway, at the risk once again of being accused of blowing my own trumpet, I can only say that I did not find Stowting difficult, and the previous year I had made a non-stop climb there with my high-geared, untuned series " T " M.G. Yet Stowting used to stop quite a lot of cars, and certainly it looks formidable. It is the tunnel type of hill—that is to say, it goes up between high banks and is almost entirely closed in by overhanging trees. Again I think it is mostly a case of getting sufficient road speed on the short take-off, and on a muddy get-away road speed and engine speed can be two very different things.

Stowting is no great distance from Dover, and as I had to be back in Birmingham that same night, I lost no time in getting under way, but I believe that results were got out later that same evening. As I have said, only four of us were without fault—Dickie Green, who won the Visitor's Cup, Allard (with the four-seater car built for Gilson), who registered best per-formance of the day, and W. C. N. Norton and myself (first-class awards).

Very unfortunately I did not see much of the 1937 " Gloucester." It was a case of third time *un*-lucky, because I was the only competitor in the running for a Gloucester Goblet, awarded for returning a clean sheet three years in succession, but I do not imagine for one moment that I should have been successful, even if I had got to the hills : the 1937 " Gloucester " proved to be very severe. Actually what happened was that a rock split the M.G.'s oil-sump on Old Stanway, towards the end of the night section, and before a single observed section had been tackled.

It was still dark, of course, when the damage was sustained. After all of the following competitors had gone by, my passenger, enthusiastic Jack Newton of "Notwen" oils, and myself attempted to turn the car round in order to coast it back down the hill and on to the main road. Pushing and heaving, we somehow turned it, but there was an awful moment when the car started to run away from us and we dived head first over the back into the cockpit, grabbing madly for the hand-brake.

Coasting and pushing, the car was free-wheeled right down to the cross-roads where the Broadway-Winchcombe-Cheltenham main road crosses. There we decided to sit in the car, have a breather, and wait for the dawn to come up. Gradually the world came awake, shadowy figures slid by on bicycles, cocks crowed, the sky lightened. We started again, pushing and coasting, in a vain attempt to reach Winchcombe.

Eddy Goodenough had promised to try to get help out to me, but breakfast on the " Gloucester " is taken very early and there was no guarantee that Eddy would be able to get hold of anyone in the short time at his disposal, so that I thought we had better try to reach Winchcombe, and a telephone.

To get up one slope we had help from some farm labourers on their way to work, but they had to leave us again to reach their job, and finally a stretch of uphill beat us. As we rested and recovered our breath a big car bearing trade plates came over the slope, and we were rescued.

The morning was then spent sitting disconsolately about " The Plough," at Cheltenham, waiting for a new sump to come up from Abingdon. Towards lunch-time competitors began to come in from the finish of the trial. Many of them talked, not about the very difficult new hill, Breakheart, but about the new loop on Station Hill (Chalford).

I saw, and attempted, both of these hills subsequently. Breakheart is a most difficult hill, and calls for a first-class machine and driver. The second (left-hand) corner has to be judged almost to inches for a successful non-stop climb to be made. In contrast, the new loop on Station was a purely artificial obstacle, perfectly straight and very short, but very steep and with a surface of loose earth, and in the " Gloucester " competitors had to tackle this with virtually no take-off at all. Actually there were more failures here than on the very difficult Breakheart : indeed only eleven climbed, and there was a lot of discussion about it.

Juniper was not quite so lethal as in the 1936 event, but as many as thirty-nine failed out of the seventy-odd who were running, and a bag of twenty-five victims was claimed by Hodgecombe. In the end only Philip Flower and Macdermid had made non-stop ascents of every one of the eleven hills.

I am sure that no one was more pleased than Macdermid himself that, of the two of them, it should be Flower who secured the Gloucester Cup. In *The Sports Car* (January 1938) Macdermid wrote : " I was lucky enough to see Philip Flower tackle the hill (Breakheart), and I would like to pay a tribute to as clever a trials man as any that twiddles a wheel. Flower is unable to survey his hill on foot, but unerringly he picked the only possible course and quietly but very surely took his car to the top : a perfectly judged climb which made all others look rather futile."

Through my misfortune on Old Stanway I certainly missed a severe but sporting event of which the results were :

Gloucester Cup.—P. S. Flower (847 c.c. M.G.).

1100 c.c. Class.—D. J. Holliday (972 c.c. Singer).

1500 c.c. Class.—R. A. Macdermid (1292 c.c. M.G. s/c).

2000 c.c. Class.—L. G. Johnson (1911 c.c. Frazer-Nash-B.M.W.).

Unlimited Class.—G. Warburton (3622 c.c. Allard).

Second-Class Awards.—K. N. Hutchison (Ford Special) ; A. G. Imhof (M.G.) ; J. M. Toulmin (M.G.) ; W. C. N. Norton (Ford V8) ; H. G. Symmons (L.M.B.-Ford Special) ; M. H. Lawson (H.R.G.) ; C. D. Buckley (Austin) ; C. Goodacre (Austin) ; H. L. Hadley (Austin).

Third-Class Awards.—S. H. Allard (Allard) ; N. V. Terry (Frazer-Nash-B.M.W.) ; V. S. A. Biggs (Frazer-Nash-B.M.W.) ; A. B. Langley (M.G.) ; W. P. Uglow (H.R.G.) ; E. K. Farley (H.R.G.) ; E. B. Booth ($1\frac{1}{2}$-litre Singer) ; A. H. Langley (Austin) ; W. H. Scriven (Austin) ; J. F. A. Clough (Riley) ; R. K. N. Clarkson (Ford V8-L.M.B.).

CHAPTER IX

Organizing

A T this stage, winter 1937, I was a very busy little man indeed. Added to my trials activities and, of course, the inescapable necessity of earning the daily bread, I was making preparations to get married and establish a home, and was also taking a hand, along with the other members of the Midland Centre of the M.G. Car Club, in organizing a trial.

Although the Midland Centre had been the first of the separate centres of the M.G. Car Club to be established, we of the committee had, so far, fought shy of organizing a trial, mainly because of our firm conviction that the trials calendar was overloaded already. Despite this overloading, however, it became apparent that support would be forthcoming for an event, and when there were presented to the Club certain trophies of a calibre which would obviously have to be competed for in a contest of more serious type than a gymkhana, a decision was taken to organize a trial, to be held early in February 1938.

The first step, of course, was the forming of a set of regulations, nothing like such a simple business as might be supposed, and many a tankard of Flower's bitter (no connection with the redoubtable Philip) went into the compiling of those " regs." Then we got down to the question of route. It was very tempting, indeed, to take the path of least resistance and stage either a Juniper–Old Hollow affair or, possibly, a Bamford–Cowlow–Washgates scramble, but I am glad to be able to say that we resisted temptation.

It was not only a desire for originality that prompted us. Behind the scenes in the trials world things were going on again. With many sections of the public, trials had fallen into disfavour. Undoubtedly there were far too many events, although, in this particular, the motor-cycle fraternity were often thought to be bigger sinners than the organizers of car trials. Certainly there was a vast multiplicity of small motor-cycle events, and it was no uncommon thing to find several quite separate trials all converging on the same spot on the same day at the same time, usually unbeknown to each other.

Photo : "The Autocar"

1937 "ABINGDON"—J. A. BASTOCK ("MUSKETEER" M.G.) ENTERS TIN PAN ALLEY
WITH HIM IS A. E. ("JIM") FROST

1937 "GLOUCESTER."—E. H. GOODENOUGH ("BLOWN" PB M.G.) COMING
OUT OF THE FIRST CORNER ON FERRISCOURT

It was not, as a general rule, the long-distance M.C.C. classics, or the " Colmores," that caused trouble. A remarkable number of new clubs had been launched and established, and the first desire of any of these organizations seemed always to be to run a trial. While most of these clubs were second to none in their very real enthusiasm, not all of them were able to bring to bear the matured experience of such long-established clubs as, for example, Sunbac or the Motor-Cycling Club or the North-West London Club. There was many a snare and pitfall for the unwary in the organizing of road trials, and, if these were not promptly avoided, harm could soon be caused to the sport as a whole.

Not only was far too frequent use made of certain well-known hills, but it would happen, also, that because Club A used a particular hill with great success, Club B would then include this hill in the route for their trial. But, whereas Club A would probably have contacted the local council and local chief constable—or the owner, if private property—Club B, less experienced, would often assume that because Club A had used the hill it was quite in order for that hill to be used in Club B's trial, and no contact would be made with local bodies. A more imaginative get-together with local authorities, particularly the constabulary, might have eased the path quite a lot.

One could readily understand, and sympathize with, the temptation to use well-known hills rather than to attempt to strike out afresh, and possibly come a flop on the day of the trial. Just the same, by the opening of the 1938 season, trials generally were in bad odour, even to the point of questions being asked in " The House," and a threat of legislation. I think, myself, that the " nuisance value " of trials was overstated, but those whose hand was raised against us were vociferous enough to make their voices heard in places where harm could be done to our sport.

Rather naturally, therefore, we in the Midland Centre of the M.G. Car Club preferred the rather onerous task of trying to find something new, to the idea of establishing yet another trial in the Cotswolds, or Derbyshire, or perhaps the Chilterns, and aggravating an already sore position.

I cannot claim that we managed to be entirely original. The same week-end as the " Gloucester " there had been a trial of the Hagley and District Light Car Club, in an area bounded roughly, very roughly, by Bridgnorth, Ludlow, and Church Stretton, in fact, broadly, the Clee Hills. Kenneth Delingpole and Geoffrey Mansell had competed, and when the question came up as to where we should hold our trial, Delingpole suggested that this area might prove well worth exploiting, while there had, at the same time, been one hill in the Hagley Club's trial to which he certainly thought we ought to help ourselves.

So Delingpole conducted us to The Yeld, on the lower slopes of Brown Clee Hill, close by the little village of Clee St. Margaret. We liked The Yeld ; one or two most cheery Sunday mornings were passed there. There was one drawback to the hill : it was mainly grass, and had the inherent fault of its type that on a really dry day it would almost certainly lose its sting completely.

It was far from dry on our first visit there, and our first attempts to climb were unavailing, though the cause of much entertainment to an enthusiastic audience of about six locals. Cyril, their red-headed ringleader, proved to be a " proper lad," and proceeded to encourage us to further effort by trotting off to a near-by farmhouse and returning with a large jug of " climbing ale " (parsnip wine). Thus fortified, I persuaded the " PB " to the summit, but it was obvious that, given wet weather, a reasonable expectation in February, the month in which the trial was scheduled, the hill would be a " stopper." In the Hagley Trial it had failed the entire entry, Delingpole and Mansell included. We had a number of cheerful reunions with Cyril, and finally, on the day of the trial, pressed him into service as a marshal and observer.

Yes, you can have lots of fun organizing a trial. We tried dozens of possible hills all over Shropshire, and gradually we built up our course. You can run into some awkward situations too.

We had given Alan Hunt the job of clerk of the course, since his flair for organization was a byword, and one Sunday he came along and announced that he had found a hill. It was in the right district to match in with the course we were planning and we went along to *vet*. the new " find."

The good metalled lane on which we approached deteriorated suddenly, after passing under an iron footbridge, into a quagmire of liquid mud with appalling ruts. We left the cars and proceeded on foot. A little way on was a fork, from which point both tracks rose sharply. The explanation of the wicked condition of he approach to this point was at once evident. The track to the left led into a wood, in which extensive timber-felling was in progress, and the fallen timber was evidently being got out, dragged by tractors, along the track up which we had come.

The track to the right from the fork was the one Hunt had thought looked promising, and we agreed with him. Although timber had been felled at the sides, it had not, apparently, been dragged down the track, the surface, so far as we walked, seeming to be in good order. Unfortunately there was no other approach to this right-hand track than the sea of mud and ruts, and, reluctantly, we had to agree that the approach, in its present condition, was scarcely a fair obstacle, and that we might, indeed, get the whole trial completely bogged there were we to attempt to use it.

All the same, we could not get the hill off our minds, and so, the next Sunday, it was decided to take two cars, Bastock's " Musketeer " M.G. and my blown ex-" Cream Cracker " M.G. and enter the hill from the top. After careful study of the map we set out, and eventually found our way on to the hill. It was then discovered that, on the upper reaches, a deal of timber had been felled and a lot was stacked at the side of the track, so that, in places, there was barely room to get past. There was some discussion, if we went down we could not come back up that way : the hill was of the type on which a good road speed would have had to be maintained to climb successfully, and the stacked tree branches made the track too narrow to risk trying to climb at speed. If we went on down, it meant that we would have to go all the way, traverse the quagmire, and get out to the bottom of the hill. We decided to have a go. It was an unwise decision.

Both cars stuck fast. There was nothing for it but to try to dig out. Not one of us had a pair of gum-boots, and in a matter of seconds we were soaked to the knees with ice-cold water and squelching mud. The light was failing fast also by this time. Somehow we levered Bastock's car out at last, but mine resisted all efforts to shift it.

Finally, shivering, soaking wet, the daylight all but gone, we slogged through the mud down into the village to try to get a horse. After some delay we were successful in our quest, and, in darkness now, the " PB " was rescued. Unfortunately, wet feet have an immediate reaction on my stupidly delicate tummy, and, despite drying-out sodden shoes and mud-caked socks before a roaring fire at the nearest pub, and knocking back neat brandies to try to stave off chill, I began to feel ill almost at once, and I was a most definite liability to my fellow committee men that evening. I was not even able to drive my car home, a task I had to pass over to Frank Kemp, while I huddled in the passenger's seat.

"Hunt's Horror," as we had immediately dubbed this hill, did eventually get used in a trial. Sunbac included it in the route of their 1938 Vesey Cup Trial, under its proper name of Eaton Hill.

We were very undecided, at first, whether to include in our route the hill (!) we named "Allez 'Oop" : in fact, we all but passed it by without even giving it a trial.

Allez 'Oop is a purely artificial obstacle, being little more than a deep cleft in the side of the Long Mynd. We had passed a number of similar fissures in the hillside, but something about this particular one prompted further investigation. Investigation revealed that Allez 'Oop had that little something that the others didn't possess. It did peter out and lose itself on the hillside finally, like the others, but it went very much farther before so doing, and was drivable all the way. While most of the other clefts went straight up, and were either too narrow, too rocky, or too suddenly steep, Allez 'Oop had a good right-hand right-angle corner, and a non-damaging surface.

The hill is a long way from anywhere ; there is virtually no traffic on the secondary lane that runs at its foot, and a trial might easily have passed that way without anyone unconnected with the event having knowledge of it. Just the same, we went to work to find out to whom that property belonged, and obtained written permission, readily granted, for its use. The little bit of trouble involved was always well worth while.

For the "Exeter," which, in point of fact, was not the last trial of 1937, but the first of 1938, falling on January 7th and 8th, the Motor-Cycling Club revived two hills which had not figured in the "Exeter" route for some years, Higher Rill and Wood-haynes, and also included Knowle Lane, in Dorset, the finish being moved from Blandford to Bournemouth.

"An Easier 'Exeter'" ran *The Autocar* headline (January 14th, 1938), and, in respect of the comparative straightforward-ness of the hills, it was justified. Midlanders started, as had now become customary, from Stratford on Avon, proceeding through

Bidford on Avon to Evesham, and later picking up the main Bristol road at Tewkesbury. Between Stratford and Bidford there is one of those gradual curves (left-handed) which " keeps on going round." I know the spot well.

In the middle of the corner Macdermid, leading the " Musketeer " M.G.s, suddenly found his car going out of control on an unexpected patch of ice. The car went up on the grass verge, which is very wide at this point, and capsized. Bastock and Langley, following closely, never had a chance. To have attempted to brake suddenly on the ice patch would have been suicidal : they could only struggle to take " avoiding action." Langley was fortunate : his car spun wildly, but stayed on the road and was undamaged, but Bastock's went up on the grass and hit a telegraph pole. Other competitors were soon on the scene and willing hands were quickly at work sorting the " Musketeers " out. Macdermid and his passenger were found to be not seriously hurt, and, apart from the complete smashing of the windscreen, the car had suffered only superficial damage to the " top hamper." Macdermid elected to continue, Langley also, though this was not possible for Bastock, who limped painfully home through the night, the car only just drivable.

Dickie Green was also eliminated by an accident. Green, Goodenough, and myself were travelling in sequence, and had entered as a team. Being presumed to know the locality, I took the lead, but, being overtired, I took a wrong turning after Evesham, and had gone quite some distance before realizing my error, Green and Goodenough, of course, following me.

I called a halt, set a fresh direction, and started off again, not appreciating that Green was not following. He, apparently, had got out of his car momentarily, and had not realized that Goodenough and myself were off again, until he found himself being left behind. Not wanting to let us out of his sight, as he was none too sure of where we were, he shot after us, came into a corner very fast, and hit a bank at the roadside. We pulled up under a street-lamp, in Tewkesbury, and one glance was sufficient to show that the little green car could not go on : one front wheel pointed in quite a different direction to the other. I felt terribly guilty ; if I had not taken that wrong turning, this would not have happened. Goodenough and I took an unhappy farewell of Green and his passenger, Bud Murkett, in the deserted main street of Tewkesbury, and went on.

It was an unhappy event for me altogether. In point of fact I should have been better advised not to have competed at all. Before ever I started I was overtired, having had a wearing and rather nerve-racking time trying to get my new home finished and equipped in time for my forthcoming wedding, and I felt ill throughout the trial. At the breakfast stop, indeed, I was prepared for instant and painful death, and was unable to chew even a piece of toast.

The already quoted headline from *The Autocar*, " An Easier ' Exeter,' " sums up the rest of the story, their sub-title telling you, " Fingle and Simms Not Quite Up to Form. 84 out of 180 Starters Claim Premier Awards."

Higher Rill was used as a re-start hill, while Woodhaynes and Knowle Lane offered plenty of mud, lashings of it, in fact, but little real gradient.

Two of the first people I met on arrival at Bournemouth were Dickie Green and Bud Murkett. Dickie had crawled on as far as Gloucester, and there had knocked up an hotel and secured accommodation for what remained of the night. Murkett's folk were the Rover agents in Bedford, and in the morning a 'phone call was put through to Bedford, the " family " Rover was brought down to Gloucester, and Green and Murkett turned up at the finish of the " Exeter " after all.

Macdermid and Langley both gained premier awards, after their adventure in the night.

Shortly afterwards I had another taste of the " Lawrence " hills, this time under winter conditions, going down to Bagshot Heath for a trial of the Sunbeam Motor-Cycle Club. The weather was threatening throughout, though this threat did not actually materialize, and cold. I did not get quite such a kick from it as I had done from the 1937 " Lawrence." The brilliant weather on that occasion had certainly played some part in making that particular event one of my happiest.

The short, sharp, sudden, and loose-surfaced hills were still a thrill. There was one really fierce new one, of which the final few yards appeared to be completely vertical, with a surface like the sands of the desert. Not even Allard could manage it.

Not far away the M.G. Car Club was running its annual Chilterns Trial. The winner was D. E. (Dave) Harris. Harris had " swapped horse " again, and now had one of the trials-modified series " T " M.G.s.

Change was in the air. The two M.G. teams had new cars also. These were still, basically, the series " T " model, but the new " Crackers " had the 12 h.p., 1550 c.c. engine in the Midget chassis, while the three new " Musketeer " cars had supercharged engines. In both teams increased ground-clearance had been obtained at the front, by the front springs being set up with a steep camber. Big, piston-type Luvax shock absorbers were fitted all round, and pressed-steel oil-sumps were used again, instead of the more vulnerable cast-aluminium. The gear-boxes were not interfered with this time.

Godfrey Imhof also had one of the 12 h.p.-engined cars, and struck an altogether original note by having the spare-wheel bracket fixed in front of the radiator.

Hutchison, who, during the latter half of 1937, had been carving a very definite niche for himself with the special, spidery Ford, started the 1938 season with an Allard Special. Whereas the power unit of Allard's own car had always been a 30 h.p. V8 Ford engine (since it was from a Ford that the Allard had been evolved), Hutchison decided to have his car driven by one of the much more powerful V12, 40 h.p. Lincoln engines.

An even more elaborate, specially built car, based on the now ubiquitous V8 Ford, was that being driven in trials by H. G. Symmons, 1935 " Experts " winner. It was known as an L.M.B. Special, after its designer, L. M. Ballamy. At the other end of the scale was a remarkable machine driven by D. G. Flather, basically a 1½-litre Brescia Bugatti, of most uncertain vintage.

On Sunday, February 13th, the Midland Centre of the M.G. Car Club held its first trial. The date was unlucky for us in but one respect, that of the weather. The gentle rains from heaven, which we had felt it reasonable to expect in the month of February, were conspicuously absent. It was very dry and very cold, so that even our " exclusive horror," the exciting-looking Allez 'Oop, stopped but a mere nineteen of the forty-seven starters, and car after car treated The Yeld as a speed hill-climb. I could have wept as I thought back to that first morning when Bastock, Delingpole, and myself literally flung ourselves at the mud and ruts of the first corner, time and again spinning, churning, and sliding to a standstill.

I was fortunate in being able to see performances on all of our hills on the day of the trial, as I had the congenial task of travelling from point to point on the course conveying E. P. Willoughby, Midlands editor of *The Light Car*, who was covering the event for his paper. The opportunity had not presented for Willoughby to ride in a "trials special" for quite a time, and after he had settled down to the clatter of the straight-cut crown-wheel, and I had fixed him up with an old leather coat, he enjoyed the outing no end, writing several paragraphs about it in his "Rich Mixture" article in the following Friday's issue of *The Light Car*.

The trial was a triumph for our very good friends and sporting rivals, the "Grasshopper" Austins. These were the results :

Bryant Cup.—A. H. Langley (747 c.c. Austin s/c).
Ludlow Cup.—C. D. Buckley (747 c.c. Austin s/c).
Committee Cup.—F. D. Gilson (3622 c.c. Allard).
Grasshopper Cup.—W. H. Depper (747 c.c. Austin s/c).
Kimber Team Trophy.—Buckley, Langley, W. H. Scriven.
Inter-Centre Team Award.—J. Terras, K. A. Scales, J. Twyford (N.-W. Centre).

Nine first-class and as many as thirty-two second-class awards were won.

CHAPTER X

1938

TO intrude a purely personal note, on the following Wednesday, February 16th, I married Joan Edmonds at Harborne Parish Church (Birmingham), firmly supported by Dickie Green in the rôle of best man. Except that morning-coats were worn instead of leather coats, the reception resembled nothing so much as the start of a " Land's End." I have since been assured, on many an occasion, that a *very* " good time was had by all."

I was a bit shaken when I heard that Warren Hill was to be included in the route for the 1938 " Colmore." I wondered if any car would succeed in climbing it. I knew Warren from having observed there during the motor-cycle " Colmore." It is nothing more than a footpath in a wood, with a surface of beaten earth. It narrows at the top, to culminate in a gateway wide enough only for the passage of a motor-cycle. In the car trial it was approached from the opposite direction to that usually taken by the motor-cyclists, which involved the negotiation of a sharp and slippery hairpin with strongly adverse camber, before getting on to the main part of the hill.

On the day of the trial remarkable scenes were witnessed there. Car after car continued to go straight ahead after the steering wheels had been locked hard over to take the cars into the corner. The surface on the corner itself was like a skating rink. Engines raced, tyres threshed madly at the greasy earth, until smoke rose from them, drivers and passengers bounced hectically up and down in their seats in unavailing efforts to aid non-existent wheel-grip—and Allard, with a new car, Warburton in the original Allard, CLK 5, and T. H. Cole, driving a " Grasshopper " type, blown Austin, showed that the track was climbable.

I was frankly disappointed when my car registered another failure, at Juniper. Green had climbed non-stop, immediately in front of me, and I had expected to do the same, but it was not to be. Actually, I failed in good company. Juniper proved to be the second most difficult hill in the trial, failing all but

fourteen. Among the failures was Cole's little Austin, one of
the three conquerors of Warren, so that, in the end, only Allard
and Warburton finished " clean " (!)

What a " needle-match " these two had for the Trophy. In
the tie-deciding driving test, at the cross-roads by Guiting Wood,
both drivers returned exactly the same times ! The decision lay
on the figures for the other special test, at Lypiatt, and as a result
of this, Warburton won the 1938 " Colmore " by the narrow
margin of just one-fifth of a second ! Thus the car on which
Allard himself had won the 1937 " Colmore " now made best
performance of the day in the 1938 trial in Warburton's hands.

To complete the " Colmore " story, Leckhampton seemed to
be losing its sting. My car romped up, and so did many others,
so that the hill was conquered by more than twice as many cars
as got up Juniper—thirty-four in all.

Green, who had been winning awards right and left since the
beginning of the year, secured the Rhode Cup. Of the others
who climbed Juniper, Buckley (" Grasshopper " Austin) took the
Shell Cup ; Scriven (with the second of the " Grasshopper "
Austins) was best in the 750 c.c. Class ; Philip Flower in the
1100 c.c. Class ; Toulmin, leading the new 12 h.p.-engined
" Cream Cracker " cars, in the 2000 c.c. Class ; and Hutchison,
on the big Lincoln-engined Allard, the Unlimited Class. H. G.
Symmons (Ford-engined L.M.B.-Special) won the " Cream
Crackers" award (for a driver never having won a first-class award
or better in a Colmore Trial) ; Crawford, Jones, and M. S.
Soames (Ford V8) collected the only three second-class awards
given, while W. H. Depper (blown Austin), the fourteenth of the
Juniper climbers, had the misfortune to fail on Leckhampton,
and had to be satisfied with a third-class award.

The rush of events never slackened ; trial followed trial in
bewildering sequence. Yet each drew its measure of support,
though often that measure was less than thirty cars, each had its
own particular atmosphere, each provided its own particular
incidents, and rarely were any two events of exactly the same
pattern, even though many ran over much the same ground.

The weather, of course, was often a dominating factor, so
that, in reporting the Great West Motor Club's Spring Cup
Trial, *The Light Car* (March 25th, 1938) used the headlines :
" Dry but Difficult. Great West M.C. Bournemouth Trial Loses
Nothing by Fine Spell."

Although it was but a couple of weeks into March, there was nothing to distinguish the day from one in midsummer. A brazen sun shone down, unblinking, from a cloudless, deep blue sky. The " business end " of the route was laid on the Tank Corps test grounds at Bovington Camp, Wool Heath (Dorset), an area providing hills almost identical with the " Lawrence " hills at Bagshot Heath and Frimley.

This is about the only type of trials hill which tends to become more difficult when dry. A little rain will usually have the effect of binding together the fine, loose sand of which the surfaces of these hills are formed, but when really dry the sand sifts into a fine powder in which frantic wheelspin is rapidly provoked. So that, whereas the West of England Motor Club's trial, away in Devon on the Saturday—won by Macdermid, with the team award to the " Grasshopper " Austins, and cups for Buckley, Langley (Alf), Bastock, Hutchison, and J. E. West (H.R.G.)— proved " unexpectedly easy " (*The Sports Car*, May 1938) because of the dry spell, in the Sunday's trial at Bovington Camp clean sheets were at a premium. M. S. Soames (Ford V8) was the Spring Cup winner, E. K. Farley (H.R.G.) best in opposite class, and the Visitor's Spring Cup fell to L. G. Johnson (B.M.W.), with D. P. Kirkman (Alvis) best in opposite class. Kirkman's Alvis was the machine of uncertain vintage with which, in the previous autumn, he had won the West Hants Club's Knott Trophy, and was described at that point.

Dry weather again took the sting out of the Liverpool Motor Club's Jeans Cup Trial, held in the Buxton area, and although there was a most likeable new hill, Flash Bottom, with a mud and grass surface instead of rocks, the destination of the principal awards was decided entirely by the times in the special tests. Guy Warburton won the race, and I managed to break a rather uninspiring sequence of third-class awards at last, to secure the Wade Cup (best in opposite class). " Musketeer " Langley was best visitor, Gilson (Allard) best member, with first-class awards going to Allard himself, Jim Frost, now participating regularly, and R. J. Richardson with a "Grasshopper"-type Austin Seven.

The sun shone again on the " Land's End." Eddy Goodenough and Dickie Green and myself had arranged to run in sequence, and to have a crack at that much-coveted prize, the Land's End Team Award.

What fun it is to run a team, particularly when you have

three almost identical cars, which was, of course, the case with our three blown " PB " M.G.s. We meticulously maintained numerical order throughout, and tackled every hill with the cars in sequence. There was nothing in the least original or unusual in this : it was a standard practice with the established regular teams, such as the " Cream Crackers " or the " Grasshoppers," to make a one-two-three performance, and always had been, so why it was that all three of the leading weekly motoring journals appeared positively to have gone out of their way to pick out us three for special mention in their reports of the " Land's End," we never really found out.

The Motor (April 20th, 1938) set the ball rolling with :

" The crowd was immense, very good tempered, and restrained on the steepest section by stout fences on each side of the road (Beggar's Roost). May, Green, and Goodenough, in the supercharged M.G. Midgets, were the star turn of the day. They whistled their way to the top in a cloud of stones and a crescendo of sound."

The Light Car's version of the same scene read :

" Full marks for meteoric ascents amid a shower of flying stones and clouds of dust—ascents that made the crowd roar— must be given to . . . C. A. N. May, W. J. Green, and E. H. Goodenough (M.G. Midgets P.B. s/c). . . ."

At Barton Steep we were picked out again as being " very neat," and at Darracott we figured in a short list of names of whom the report said : " They treated the hill with such disdain that it looked like a main road."

The Autocar (April 22nd) " did us proud " at Hustyn, of which hill they said : " Hustyn was in a fairly difficult condition, the lower part being dry and loose and the upper part muddy and rough. The main difficulty was a rocky outcrop about half-way up ; if a car succeeded in passing over this, a clean climb usually followed." Our passage there was described : " C. A. N. May, E. H. Goodenough, and W. J. Green—all driving supercharged M.G.s—were all very fast, sliding the bends on the lower slopes." *The Light Car* went nap and used " excellent " as their description of our climbs on Hustyn !

Phew ! After all that, little wonder that we had to endure much pointed, but always good-natured, leg-pulling, usually on the lines that what a pity it was we had not been able to persuade the press that our photos should appear !

Anyway, whatever the reason for our fine press notices, they tell the story of the sort of " Land's End " we three had. I have always had a specially soft spot in my heart for the " Land's End," and, indeed, between 1933, when I did my first " Land's End " as passenger with H. K. Crawford, and the outbreak of war I never missed the M.C.C.'s Easter classic. To have gone through the 1938 event in such style, and to have been able to enjoy, throughout, the cheery company of my friends and their passengers (John Siddall, M.G. Car Club S.W. Centre secretary, was with Green,. Eddy's sister, Mary, was with him as always, my wife rode with me) naturally leaves this particular trial as one of my very happiest trials memories.

Yet, although we could not know it at the time, disaster was only round the corner. I had taken a risk, a small one in my opinion, but even so unjustifiable really, with our hearts so set on the Team Award, but it was in deference to my wife. Being still not reconciled to the clatter of the straight-cut teeth of my special crown-wheel and pinion, she had asked if the " Land's End " could not be safely accomplished on an ordinary, quiet back-end, for, after all, there were no hectic driving tests of the type in which sudden and violent changes of direction, from forwards to reverse, are called for, and even the much-discussed re-start on Crackington was not to be repeated, this hill being taken as a straight climb. Nothing was known of the new hill that was to figure in the route, New Mill, near Boscastle, but by the very nature of the Land's End Trial one knew that it could not be of the Juniper calibre.

It seemed a reasonable enough request, and when the opportunity presented to pick up a complete, made-up, differential assembly, with the normal type of spiral-bevel crown-wheel and pinion in place, thus facilitating a quick change-over, I met my wife's wishes.

As seems always to occur in these cases, the change-over was not made until the last minute, actually on the Thursday, and but a cursory examination made of the spare assembly. Asking for trouble, of course, and I got it, but not, by the greatest good fortune, on the " Land's End." It was on the final hill in Sunbac's inter-team trial, the following Saturday, that the crown-wheel stripped, so that not a tooth was left whole. After Lloyd-Jones had stripped and examined the differential assembly he said that he was satisfied, from his examination, that the crown-wheel had never been locked up properly, and the supporting ball-races had been slowly undoing themselves all through the Land's End Trial and subsequently !

That this little break-up was round the corner could not, of course, be known to the six of us who drank happily to a successful " Land's End," after signing the finishing sheet and confidently claiming our P.A.s (Premier Awards).

I will admit, frankly, that we believed the Team Award to be " in the bag," but there is many a slip 'twixt the cup and the lip. With the publication of the official results it was found that the team award had gone to the "Grasshopper" Austins (Buckley, Scriven, Langley). Hurriedly I checked down the list. " E. H. Goodenough (13E)—no award." What on earth was 13 ? Here it is—" Early at intermediate time-check." It was difficult to see how this could have happened without Green and myself also being at error with our time-keeping, and we queried the point, but the M.C.C. records were clear that Eddy had passed the check early, even though it could not be explained how, and our cherished hopes of the Land's End Team Award could not be realized.

Before these results were actually published the " Grasshopper " boys had achieved a further success, winning Sunbac's inter-team trial, and what a party that turned out to be. The Sunbac lads had really " gone to town " in exploiting the Herefordshire area, and had gone right into the foothills of the Black Mountains, on the Welsh border.

The weather was fine again at the start, though it deteriorated later, and Pont-y-Weston proved fairly straightforward, but beyond the top Sunbac had set out the relay driving test, and on a surface mainly of grass there was tremendous fun and games. T. C. Wise gave the most thorough of several exhibitions of hedging and ditching, but performances were really capped by Norman Terry. As the B.M.W. came down fast to the finishing line, swerving the curves, it suddenly right about turned, whereupon Terry, nothing daunted, snapped in reverse and shot over the line backwards, and there was nothing in the regulations to rule him out of order.

But the crux of the team trial was Red Daren. Here is Sunbac's own description of their hill, as published in the June 1938 issue of the *Sunbac News* :

" . . . Actually it is up the open hillside of the Black

Mountains, which hereabouts rises 700 feet in as many yards, which gives some idea of the steepness. As the winding track was virtually indistinguishable from the rest of the grass-grown hillside, the route to be taken . . . was marked out with cards.

" From the starting line the track curved away right-handed to an acute left-hand hairpin, thence on a slightly lesser gradient to a right-hand hairpin, where the surface was very bumpy. From this point the track went practically straight up the side of the mountain—the ' Observed Section Ends ' notice being a few yards short of a cross-track. . . .

" It should be explained that the hill was of the ' graduated penalty ' variety, divided into five sections ' A ' to ' E.' ' A ' finished about half-way to the first hairpin. ' B ' included the first of the hairpins, but stopped short of the second one, which was in ' C,' a short section, as was also ' D.' ' E ' was a long section. . . .

" Sunbac ' A ' team were the first arrivals and Norman Terry was the first competitor to tackle the hill, but his B.M.W. would only take him as far as the first hairpin and then died on him with petrol starvation.

" Other teams, consisting of M.G.s, B.M.W.s, Singers, Austins, Allards, etc., had rather better fortune, but mostly came to rest in section ' C ' on the bumpy part just after the right-hand hairpin, although nearly a dozen attempts ended in section ' D.'

" T. H. Cole (Sunbac ' B ') looked like getting as far as ' E,' but just couldn't make it.

" The way various competitors, particularly Austen May, hurled their cars round the hairpin in attempting to collect sufficient knots to carry them over the bumps was most spectacular and rather alarming to those standing anywhere near.

" Some delay was caused in getting Clarkson's Ford off the track, as in turning the car round a tyre suddenly deflated.

" The last team to arrive was the Worcestershire Austin Owners' Club (the ' Grasshoppers '), who subsequently proved to be the winners, and when Buckley was only able to persuade his car into section ' D ' it looked as though Red Daren was not going to be conquered, but Bill Scriven got round the second hairpin and through the rough stuff with sufficient urge left to carry him about half-way through the last section—a magnificent effort.

" Alf Langley's was the last attempt of the day, and taking the right-hand hairpin rather slower than most, he just kept on motoring until he passed the ' Observed Section Ends·' notice. A truly remarkable climb and one that was loudly acclaimed by his team-mates and other spectators on his return to the foot of the hill."

And that was Red Daren, although pages and pages could be written about it, and even then it has to be seen really to be believed.

At the Hill Lane re-start the crown-wheel stripped, as already described. Goodenough and myself had been teamed with T. H. Cole (" Grasshopper "-type Austin) for this event, Green joining up with John Haesendonck and Dave Harris to run for the North-West London Motor Club. Cole had gone ahead before I suffered my breakage, but Goodenough was right behind me. He at once withdrew from the trial and insisted on towing me all the way back to my home on the outskirts of Birmingham, although his home was the far side of Bristol, a Good Samaritan act for which I remained for ever in his debt.

Things went remarkably well as far as Worcester, but after that the towing rope broke consistently and persistently, and the passenger (not my wife) and myself were terribly cold around the legs, deprived of the heat of the engine.

It was with the team trial that the old ex-" Cracker " started a puzzling period of local overheating, with most disastrous effects on plugs, a problem never completely solved. I put in a brand new set of LA 11's at the start of the " Abingdon," and they " died " on me at lunch-time the following day !

The " Abingdon " gave promise of being a really severe event ; Breakheart, Hodgecombe, Ashmeads, and Juniper were all on the route-card, but circumstances conspired against secretary Mit Harris.

Another spell of fine dry weather rendered even Juniper almost innocuous, leaving only Breakheart as a " stopper." Dickie Green went first and climbed non-stop, as he had done in the " Gloucester." I followed and stopped above the second corner, the radiator water boiling badly. After me, car after car failed on the hill, as we learned afterwards, and then Kenneth Delingpole, the blown " PB " going great guns, took the corner

Photo : "The Moor"

1938 "BARNSTAPLE."—W. J. ("DICKIE") GREEN, DRIVING "ARAMIS," OF THE 1937
"MUSKETEER" M.G. TEAM, CLIMBS DOVERHAY

1939 BLACKPOOL RALLY—K. C. DELINGPOLE (1496-c.c. H.R.G.) IN ONE OF THE "SPECIAL" TESTS

a shade too wide, got the offside wheels up the bank on the outside of the corner, and was unable to hold the car from rolling over. Delingpole was unhurt, though much shaken, but the passenger (by sheer chance it was not Mrs. D.) suffered a broken collar-bone.

A good deal of delay ensued, and finally it was decided to abandon the hill, so that the destination of the principle awards had to be decided on the times returned in the three special tests. Two of these were again sited at the Witney aerodrome, and on much the same lines as in the previous year. The third, however, was rather unusual. The start of the trial had been moved back to the M.G. factory at Abingdon, and on a rough, oval track in the grounds, cars had to average 15 m.p.h. for a short distance, accelerate to the next point, and again average 15 m.p.h. to the finish.

The M.G. Challenge Trophy was won by Kenneth Rawlings, on a lightened J2-type M.G. Cheery, light-hearted Ken Rawlings had been on a number of events with me as passenger, and was an enthusiast of the first water, and known to all the Midlands drivers. Dennis Buckley recorded the best visitor's performance, and Macdermid and L. M. Ballamy (blown, modified Ford 10) won the over and under 1100 c.c. awards respectively. Twenty-two people collected firsts.

At the summit of Juniper, Green and I were met by Goodenough. The previous year Eddy had won the Mid-Surrey Club's Grand Cup Trial, and in preparing to attempt to defend his " pot," had been practising special tests in a big field at the side of his house. AHT 1, however, had objected to the treatment and the gear-box had disintegrated.

Goodenough was still able to attempt to defend his trophy, through the very good graces of Macdermid, who also had his home in Bristol. On hearing of Goodenough's accident, Macdermid immediately came forward with an offer of the loan of his " Musketeer " car for Eddy to drive in the trial, an act for which Goodenough could not adequately express his gratitude. It would have been nice to have been able to write the required happy ending to this little episode, but the " Musketeer " suddenly took charge on a muddy *downhill* section and slid gently into a ditch, albeit without suffering any harm, but the section was observed and the Grand Cup found a new owner !

On May 28th another " Lawrence " came round, but I was still grappling with my wretched overheating problems, which seemed singularly reluctant to respond to any known treatment, and my tremendously enjoyable and always-to-be-remembered scrap with Dickie Green in the 1937 " Lawrence " could not be repeated. Green, curiously, almost exactly repeated his previous year's performance, being runner-up, not this time to the winner of the Lawrence Cup, this being won by a car in the " big " class, L. G. Johnson's B.M.W., but to the winner of the Ripley Trophy, Ernest Haesendonck.

CHAPTER XI

" Plain " Tyres

I MISSED the M.C.C.'s Torquay Rally being away on holiday at the time, and my next event was the " Barnstaple," held on August Bank Holiday Saturday.

By kind invitation of the Goodenough family, my wife and myself were spending the week-end at their home at Redhill, on the Bristol–Bridgwater road.   We travelled down to Redhill on the Friday evening, and did the rest of the trip through to Dunster early on the Saturday morning, accompanied by Goodenough, with his father in the passenger's seat.

I thought, just at first, that there was going to be a repeat of the scorching Bank Holiday week-end of 1937, but the early morning burst of sunshine was short lived.

The trial ambled gently along, in true holiday spirit, until Tarr Steps Hill was reached, and there a shock was experienced. Tarr was genuinely difficult (standard tyres were being used).

It was not uncommon in the " Barnstaple " for competitors to reach some of the hills before the observers were in position, and such was the case at Tarr.   Not that anyone worried : the foot of Tarr is a pleasant enough spot in all conscience to while away a little time.   Also, a measure of what I believe theatrical and professional folk call " light relief " was provided by Dave Harris, who just could *not* get his series " T " M.G. up Tarr that day, making three full-scale but unavailing attempts while waiting for the officials, each more lurid than its predecessor.

With the observers in position Harris made his " official " run—and failed !   Dickie Green was next away, and " made the grade."   Green had on order a new, supercharged, competition-equipped, series " T " Midget, and was disposing of both his blown " PB," MJ 9898, and also his unblown, 1937 series " T " BBM 1.   The new car was not quite ready, and there had been loaned to Dickie, for this event, A. B. Langley's car of the 1937 " Musketeer " team, ABL 965.

Yes, Tarr certainly put a kick into the 1938 " Barnstaple," failing almost exactly half the entry, twelve out of twenty-five. Many of those who did climb had very anxious moments.   I

know that I did.   I collected second (*i.e.* changed up from bottom
gear to second gear) on the lower slopes, but was unable to hang
on to the higher gear all the way.   It seems, from what I was
told, that I chose the worst possible point to change down again,
right on some greasy rock slab, but after some wheelspin that
drew smoke from the tyres, I managed just to get away with it.

I watched Bastock and his passenger, Johnny Block, literally
bounce the red " Musketeer " M.G. to the top, driving wheels
threshing madly, so that it seemed that failure was inevitable.
But they pulled through.   Block, in particular, was on the point
of exhaustion from the physical effort of bouncing up and down
in his seat to try to aid wheel-grip.

A little farther on was an unusual special test.   The test had
to be carried out in third gear (top on a three-speed box), and a
rolling start of about 40 yards was allowed, to get going so as to
cover the first section, from " A " to " B," in not *less* than
20 seconds.   The remaining distance of the test, from " B " to
" C," had to be covered as fast as possible.   Even more competitors were penalized on this than had failed on Tarr, so that,
in the end, only Green, Bastock, and myself were credited with
clean sheets, Green winning the race.   A bit bumpy and dusty,
but in the " Barnstaple " tradition, and an eminently suitable
kick-off to a Bank Holiday week-end.

I was down at Bristol again the following Saturday.   The
South-Western Centre of the M.G. Car Club had transferred
their driving tests from the car park of the football ground at
Weston-super-Mare to the car park of the Knowle Greyhound
Racing Stadium at Bristol.   It was a much smaller party than
in the previous year and the organization almost a family affair,
Eddy Goodenough time-keeping, Mary recording those times,
and Goodenough senior observing the starts and finishes.

It was run on what I consider myself to be the ideal lines for
this type of event, provided always that it is not actually raining.
All competitors completed the first test before a start was made
at all on the second test, that in its turn being completed before
the third test was brought into operation.   In this way each
competitor, if he so wishes, can watch the performances of all
other competitors.   With a very big entry, of the type received
in the National Rallies, this method cannot be adopted because
of the time factor, and a site for tests must be chosen so that all
tests can be set up and be in operation concurrently, competitors

taking all tests in succession, going straight from one to the next without pause.

I have always felt that there was more scope for this type of event, particularly with more and ever more obstacles being placed in the way of organizing road events, although I appreciate that for the proper enjoyment of these gyrations fine weather is desirable, a thing unpredictable in this sceptred isle, and also, although they can be very good fun, there is no thrill quite equal to that of breasting Widlake when all around you have failed.

I had suffered a wicked ride down from Birmingham to Bristol : rarely do I remember getting so hopelessly tied up in impenetrable traffic jams. Nevertheless, grappling with the holiday crowds seemed to have keyed me up, and for the very first time, and, as it proved, the last, I actually made fastest time of the day in a series of driving tests, with a clear two seconds' margin over Macdermid.

A couple of weeks later the Singer Motor Car Club staged an ambitious affair, of similar type, in Victoria Park, Leamington Spa. The Singer people also ran their tests one at a time, getting each completed before starting the next, and were suitably rewarded with an afternoon of brilliant sunshine.

At first I thought, for one glorious moment, that I was going to do my stuff a second time. I returned fastest time in the first of the three tests, and was in the first four in the second. Hopes rose high, and I even began to wonder if at last, after years of effort, I was really getting a grip on this business of getting from line " A " to line " B," via, of course, pylon " C," garage " D," and probably a lot of awkwardness at " E " and " F."

Pride goeth before a fall. I fell on the final test, one of those diabolical affairs with a single " garage," set at right angles to the line of approach, which has to be first entered forwards, then in reverse, the area for manoeuvre from forwards to reverse being restricted in the extreme.

The sad story of an ill-judged reverse has been recorded for posterity on a length of 8 mm. ciné-film, the property of one, Kenneth Delingpole. It has often been trotted out ! It does show, however, that my car did not actually hit the " garage." It was my time that was wrecked, through the necessity of having to make an extra forward and reverse move to avoid fouling the barriers.

It was Godfrey Imhof who produced the consistent performance that wins this type of event, while Green, running the
" PB " again, not as yet having disposed of it, was " best under
1100 c.c.," and Arch Langley " best over 1100 c.c." It was nice
to see three other very personal friends of mine win the team
award for the Midland Centre of the M.G. Car Club—Frank
Kemp, Kenneth Delingpole, and Fred Allen.

At this point let me quote some further observations of
Macdermid's from one of his excellent monthly articles in *The
Sports Car* (September 1938) :

" The recommendations of the Standing Joint Sub-Committee
of the R.A.C. have ousted all other topics of conversation in
competition circles, the competition tyre ban being the subject
of fiercest controversy. If the adoption of these recommendations
removes the threatened danger to the very existence of trials,
then the price of our security is not exorbitant, and for such
events as the M.C.C. classics I can foresee little change.

" Such is not the case with the more severe events, the
" Gloucesters " and " Colmores " of the trials calendar, as the
organizers' problem will not merely be one of grading down
the hills. With the greatly increased susceptibility to climatic
vagaries, either one must play safe with easy courses or risk
disaster by including the type of hill which we are at present
using.

" . . . With a reversion to plain treads the advantages of
the car built for trials and trials alone are increased instead of
decreased, and my reason for saying this is weight. Total weight,
not merely power-weight ratio, has always been a factor of major
importance ; plain tyres will make it doubly so.

" Power is useless if you cannot transmit it, and when you
come to a slippery hill, the man with the least amount of motor-
car to carry up with him will get the highest."

Anyway there it was ; the fiat had gone forth, and competition
tyres were banned in trials as from the following January 1st
(1939), and August and early September usually being the
" close season " for road trials, there was plenty of time to talk
about it.

I did another couple of speed events—the Bristol Club's
Backwell Hill-Climb and the Motor Cycling Club's Annual
Members' Day Meeting at Brooklands. I met with small fortune.
The overheating problems reached major proportions at

Brooklands, a set of plugs going out in half a lap, while at Back-well, too, there was that nasty holding back sort of feeling about the car, which, although it can come from partial petrol starvation, is far more often the result of pre-ignition.

As the autumn trials season got under way some of the clubs anticipated the competition tyre ban in the organizing of their events, and at once confusion arose. What was and was not a competition tyre? What was a tyre of abnormal section? There was at least one case in which a club running a trial on plain tyres permitted the use by competing cars of Michelin's knobbly " snow-mud " tyres, since, presumably, they were not actually stamped " Sports " or " Competition," though the design of the tread left nothing to the imagination !

There was some heartburning over Dunlop's Universal cover, a tyre which, although intended by the manufacturers for motor-cycle use, was also listed in one or two sizes which fitted some of the smaller cars, and having a tread design basically similar to the Dunlop sports-car tyre, though with the knobs much shallower and nothing like so widely spaced, was undoubtedly superior to the average tread design used by the various tyre manufacturers for normal road use.

Later, after several rather fiery discussions had taken place, the R.A.C. stepped in again and clarified the position. A com-prehensive list was issued of the tread designs which were, and those which were not, permitted. A schedule was also drawn up giving the maximum tyre section to be allowed in each cubic capacity class.

First of the big autumn trials, and the first to anticipate the competition tyre ban was the M.G. Car Club North-Western Centre's Trial for the Cockshoot Trophy on September 18th.

In addition to the half-dozen or so observed hills, the organizers threw in, for good measure, two timed climbs, a re-start, a braking and acceleration test (cunningly sited where cars emerged from a water-splash), and two driving tests, one of these being im-mediately at the start of the trial, from the old Bull i' th' Thorn Hotel on the Ashbourne–Buxton road.

More was the pity, therefore, that one of the observed sections should have consisted of a downhill stretch of ploughed field, a stupid and universally unpopular affair, and that Hollinsclough (re-christened Swan Rake) and sump-smashing Cheeks should have been included. I wonder why organizers of trials in the

Buxton area, with but few exceptions, never could resist these two damaging hills.

Much of the course was new to me, although I was no stranger to the Buxton area, both of the timed climbs, for example. The first, Wettonmill, was fairly straight and was mainly a question of turning up the taps and hanging on.

Beeston Tor was a very different story. No one had told me that the lower left-hand hairpin was *not* the only corner on the hill, so that I arrived all unsuspecting and " dicing " merrily in second, at the upper right-hand hairpin. There was a lurid moment ; I had visions of overturning. However, the car bounced back on to the road and got away non-stop. The invaluable Fido was again in the passenger's seat, after a long interval ; he never said a word !

Dun Cow's Grove, where the re-start was staged, was evidently a case of the bark being worse than the bite : it looked fierce enough, but only eighteen of the sixty-four starters failed there.

Pilsbury was the most lethal of the " straight " observed hills, with a bag of twenty-three.

Amidst a welter of M.G.s it was M. H. Lawson's white H.R.G. that won the Cockshoot Trophy for best performance of the day. J. B. Terras (blown " PB ") was best N.-W. Centre member, and I managed to do my stuff well enough to collect the Alexander Duckham Prize for best M.G. member other than in N.-W. Centre. Best visitor, T. C. Wise (Ford).

I had a last-minute scramble for a passenger for the " Experts." I 'phoned Goodenough at Bristol, and through him arranged, as I thought, for John Siddall, secretary of the South-Western Centre of the M.G. Car Club, to ride with me. But somewhere between the three of us there was evidently misunderstanding, and as zero hour came up in Dunster Square, on the morning of the trial, there was no sign of Siddall.

While I was waiting around I learned with much regret that the previous evening Dickie Green, with John Haesendonck as passenger, had been involved in an accident, and that Dickie's new, blown, " Musketeer " type, white, series " T " M.G. was much damaged.

Happily I was able to get first-hand information on the crew, Green and Haesendonck both arriving at Dunster from the Somerset County Hospital as competitors were getting away in the trial. Both were very shaken and Haesendonck was heavily bandaged. Fortunately both recovered completely, but there was no Experts Trial for Green that year.

Just as I had reconciled myself to being a non-starter, some hero who had come down from Bristol to spectate, learning of my plight, offered his services as passenger. I regret that his name has escaped me.

Proceedings opened well with a successful non-stop climb of Cloutsham, but on arriving at Ditch Lane I found that my fears that this was just a pseudonym for Colly were well founded. I was now running last in the trial : having been unable to start at my proper time, I had been given a new number and sent off after the last man. Several competitors were still parked in the main lane, waiting their turn to go up to the hill for their attempt, but I learned that several cars had gone up non-stop, interestedly watched by Macdermid, who was in the rôle of spectator on this occasion.

At last my turn came. It is impossible in words adequately to describe the sensation of trying to climb Colly. The nearest simile I can draw is that of being in a small rowing-boat in a very rough sea, with strong cross-currents, and I can but refer you to Macdermid's own conclusions, drawn from the observations he made there that day :

" . . . but still the most shattering thing in trials land, I can only confirm that in no other event would such an obstacle be legitimate. Actually three other sections took greater toll, but Colly remains the one section that no one ever seems anxious to tackle again, and few of the successful climbs were far from the point where cars are liable to overturn."

Leaping madly from hump to hump, the old ex-" Cracker " reached the first right-hand corner, poised daintily on one rear wheel, cleared the first steep step—and the engine cut out dead. My first thought was that the main battery cable had been severed, but investigation showed this to be undamaged. Something drew my attention to the instrument panel. The twin petrol pumps fitted on the " Cracker " were controlled by separate pull-push switches on the instrument panel, instead of being automatically switched on and off by the operation of the ignition switch. Both switches were in the " off " position. Either my passenger or myself must have caught against them as we were being flung about in the car coming through the

" ditch." I switched on, pressed the starter, and the engine roared into life, and that was Colly.

I failed also on Widlake, despite an approach up the lower slopes to such purpose that one marshal went so far as to say that it was a good thing that I had failed before I broke my neck. Maybe he had not seen Colly.

After a drink at Exford we went out on to the moor for Cowcastle and Picked Stones. I think the splash had been dammed ; the depth was terrific. I wilted visibly as I saw Godfrey Imhof's M.G. all but sink beneath the waves, and if you don't believe me, come along and see a ciné-shot I took of the scene : friends who have not seen an " Experts " think it is faked !

I blanketed the radiator of my car with the tonneau cover, and as the front dipped to the water I accelerated fiercely, the customary method of negotiating water at walking speed, slipping the clutch slightly to keep the engine revving and the exhaust-pipe clear, appearing to be entirely unavailing here. The next thing I knew was that I was actually sitting in water, nearly up to my waist—a shattering moment, to put it mildly. I was so absorbed with this sudden acute personal discomfort that I hardly realized that the car had come successfully through the water, and was pulling away strongly to the hairpin non-stop.

I knew my " Experts " : I had with me a spare pair of flannels and a change of shoes and socks. Clear of the top of the hill, I nipped over a wall and did a quick change. I could do nothing for my passenger, who must have been just as wet, but he raised no voice in protest and insisted that we continue to the end of the trial.

So we passed on to the new hill, Stoke Mill. From a little village there was a descent, which in itself looked worthy of observation in an upwards direction, to a little valley which was indeed far from the madding crowd. It was at once obvious that Stoke Mill was giving trouble. Lots of competitors were still lined up waiting to make their attempt. Gradually the queue grew a little shorter, but so, too, did the daylight. I used the waiting time to change a set of plugs. The old ex-" Cracker " had gone suddenly terribly tired, seeming as though at Picked Stones it had shot its bolt. At long last, in gathering dusk, I was sent forward to the hill. The car died away on me on the lower slopes, before reaching the difficult part of the hill.

It was now nearly dark, and as I was running as last man, all the other competitors had gone on ahead. The passenger and I decided to return the way we had come. Easier said than done. The hill I had thought worthy of observation justified my opinion ; my car failed there also. The outlook was somewhat black. I reversed back and tried again, and with the passenger pushing, I at last got the car to the top, the radiator water boiling furiously, and in pitch darkness we found our way back to Blackmoor Gate.

Here are the results of the last pre-war Experts Trial :

Winner.—A. H. Langley (747 c.c. Austin s/c).
Runner-up.—M. H. Lawson (1496 c.c. H.R.G.).
1100 c.c.—C. D. Buckley (747 c.c. Austin s/c).
1500 c.c.—A. E. Frost (1490 c.c. B.M.W.).
2000 c.c.—J. M. Toulmin (1708 c.c. M.G.).
Unlimited.—S. H. Allard (3622 c.c. Allard).

CHAPTER XII

Farewell to JB 7521

THE financial aspect of regular trials participation was rearing its ugly head again. Domestic commitments, consequent upon establishing my own home, had made inroads on the family purse. Much as I was loath to have to face up to the fact, the time had come for, at least, a cutting-down of activities.

I pondered the subject long and deeply, and eventually I decided that for 1939 I would restrict myself to the long-distance M.C.C. classics, events of the calibre of the Blackpool Rally, and possibly odd holiday trials such as the light-hearted " Barnstaple." This programme had an added attraction, in that it seemed that a " milder " type of car than the old ex-" Cracker," and, therefore, one of more convenient type for the daily round, would be suitable for the undertaking of it.

So there came the decision, also, to part company with JB 7521. The old car and I had enjoyed two very happy, and not altogether unsuccessful, years together, but domestic and business commitments rather dictated my decision for me.

There came the question of a successor to JB 7521, and that, too, called for much deliberation, as it was desired to have so very much a dual-purpose motor. Finally, it was another M.G. that I decided to buy, a series " T " Midget, but fitted with the smart and snappy-looking drophead coupé bodywork recently introduced on this chassis.

With the re-start on the upper part of Bluehills prominently in mind, I arranged to have the lower bottom and second-gear ratios, as fitted on the unblown 1937 " Musketeer " and " Cream Cracker " cars, and also decided to have a slight increase in the engine compression ratio. The only other concessions I made to competition requirements were the fitting of big piston-type shock absorbers—although these made the ride a bit harsh, and later the rear pair were removed—and the positioning of the rear number-plate and tail-lamp high up on the offside rear mudguard.

Meanwhile I did my last three events on the blown " PB," the " Vesey," the " Fedden," and a trial of the Hagley Club.

It would have been nice to have been able to record that the old car went out in a blaze of glory, but unfortunately, in actual fact, rather the reverse was the case. In the " Vesey " I had one of those awful " can't-do-right " days, and achieved the doubtful distinction of failing on every hill. In the " Fedden " the car won its last award in my hands, but it was only a third-class award, failure being met on both Narkover and Juniper.

The route-card gave little indication of what lay before competitors in the " Vesey." The start had been placed at Bridgnorth. I observed, however, that The Yeld was to be used, and there seemed something familiar about the name " Eaton Hill." It was only *en route* that I realized that this was the proper name of " Hunt's Horror," where Bastock and myself had got stuck just about twelve months previously, prospecting for our M.G. Car Club Midland Centre Trial, as described in detail earlier.

The mud and ruts of the approach had eased out quite a lot, but the hill still managed to fail roughly half the entry. But at Dunstan's Lane, the next hill, and Sunbac's own special " find," a mere six competitors climbed, and only nine of the twenty-four entrants were able to make The Yeld.

Alf Langley (" Grasshopper " Austin) registered his second win in successive week-ends, the " Vesey " following right after the " Experts," although Hutchison tied with him on the driving test, and the decision rested on the timed climb, where Langley was some two seconds faster.

Hutchison's Allard was not the big, Lincoln-engined car which he had been driving all through the season, but a new job, designed for the forthcoming standard-tyre trials, and using the smaller Ford engine again.

Ford-engined specials were very much " in the air." A V8 Ford unit now powered Lloyd Jones's " Triangle Special," one of the successful six on Dunstan's in the " Vesey." Later he built up another car on similar lines, and the original " Triangle " passed into the hands of Geoffrey Mansell, who had not been active in trials for some time.

There was quite a lot of Ford, in addition to the engine, in the make-up of Norman Terry's new trials car, in which a unique note was struck by the chassis being extended *forwards*, and the front axle and wheels set out ahead of the radiator.

W. C. Butler turned up to the " Vesey " with a V8 Ford

engine under the bonnet of his old original, white, 1½-litre Singer, but had a deal of trouble with the cooling, a trouble, curiously, experienced by Allard when he evolved the first Allard Special from the T.T. Ford.

The " Fedden " well maintained the tradition it had built up for itself over the years of being a really sporting event backed by excellent organization. This time Narkover was sticky, but not so sticky as Juniper. A great many trials hills over the years seemed to lose their sting, but never could this be said of Juniper, which, except possibly in midsummer, as in the " Abingdon," remained a " stopper " to the very end.

Stancombe is a most favourite spot for special tests, usually of the timed-climb type, but the Bristol folk used it in a new way. The hill was entered from the top, and from a point just below the upper corner, competitors had to accelerate *downhill* round the corner customarily taken *uphill*, right-handed. Some distance below the corner a line had to be crossed, and then the car brought back up the hill and round the hairpin again in reverse, back to the original starting-point.

With my ciné I filmed Imhof's performance here. Speed downhill is not so easy to judge, and Imhof locks over a fraction late for the hairpin. The little white car goes right up on to the Cotswold stone wall on the outside of the corner at a tremendous angle. You draw in your breath, certain that nothing can stop the car from capsizing, and, for all that it is a length of silent film, brace yourself for the noise of the crash as the M.G. goes over. But fate is with Imhof : part of the wall dislodges, and the white car slides off with it—an exciting moment !

When the trial was over, and " buttoned up," it was found to have been another Allard day, with Warburton the winner.

High spot of the Hagley Club's Trial was to have been a number of sort of small " Rushmeres " in a field not far from the famous Red Marley motor-cycle freak hill near Witley in Worcs.

In one of the club's events in the early summer these sections had been used with great success, but on the present occasion torrential rain fell during the earlier part of the trial, and, by the time the field was reached, conditions there were so appalling that one wondered if the club would not have been better advised to have cut it out.

Extraordinary things happened, and it is a fact that at least one car, Terry's B.M.W., stuck so fast in the mud that it had to be abandoned and rescued the next day ! The majority of the competitors could not even reach the sections that had originally been marked out ; never have I seen so many cars motoring almost completely sideways, and never, never have I arrived home from an event with my clothing in such a state. What was left of my shoes had to be thrown away.

It is difficult to know just what to say about the " Gloucester." That this one-time classic went badly to pieces was undeniable. Not all of the troubles that beset the 1938 event could be construed as the fault of the organizers. There was, for example, some malicious interference with the route-marking, but it was difficult to reconcile the advance " Blurb," about coming along even if you had only a family saloon, with the including of a hill like Juniper, after the decision had been taken to run the trial on standard tyres. The " Gloucester," remember, is a December trial.

Having now disposed of the old " Cracker," and the new coupé not yet being to hand, I was enabled to go down to the Cotswolds, to see something of the " Gloucester," through the kindness of Kenneth Delingpole, who lent me his " PB " for the day.

I went first to Juniper, taking my ciné-camera. Let us run the film through. Here is Dickie Green, fit and well again, the car in good order too, turning in the gateway above the fork, after a gallant but unavailing effort. Dickie told me that both his blown " PB " and his unblown " T " were to continue appearing in trials. Bud Murkett, his former passenger, had taken over the " PB," and C. W. (Bill) Taylor, who had been doing his stuff with a 1½-litre Singer, was to drive the series " T."

Sunshine filters through the trees and slants across Biggs's English-bodied B.M.W., which looks for a moment like breaking the run of failures, but wheelspin beats it.

An oldish, skimpy-bodied Riley fails only just above the fork, but Crozier's twin-blown V8 Ford, coming up with a rush, slides to a standstill right in front of me.

Macdermid roars up hanging on to second gear until the very last moment, but the instant bottom is re-engaged, the " Musketeer " churns to a stop.

Just above where I stood a notice was fixed to the bole of a tree, " Non-Stop Continues." I wondered ! I started to pack away my camera when there was a roar and a flash from the bottom of the hill, and grabbing up my camera again, I was just able to catch M. S. Sоames's climb with the light, aluminium-bodied Allard. In the film the Allard appears to be doing about 30 m.p.h. at the point at which all the previous cars are seen coming to a standstill. Swaying from side to side, the car disappears among the trees in most alarming manner.

Just as I got back to the foot of the hill again, Guy Warburton arrived to make his attempt. Although I was not able to get. back up the hill to " shoot " him, I stayed to learn that his climb was made non-stop.

I drove across to Nailsworth, arriving just in time to get a " shot " of Norman Terry, coming up fast with the new special. A little later I had lunch with him, and he told me that the new car had performed splendidly, and realized all his hopes, although he had not managed to persuade it to the top of Juniper.

Nailsworth did not seem to be giving a lot of trouble. The sun was shining strongly ; it was more like autumn than winter. Warburton flashes up, in my film, at tremendous speed, the Allard twice leaping completely clear of the ground. It was a different story just across the Common, at Bownham. This hill runs up almost parallel with the probably better-known Ham Mill. The upper reaches are rutted and muddy, and it is a single-width track between banks. During the time I was there I was able to film only one non-stop climb, that of Soames in the big Allard. Again it is a question of road speed, the Allard coming up in a manner more reminiscent of the lower slopes of Shelsley than a muddy-surfaced trials hill.

For the third year in succession only two drivers were able to claim hundred-per-cent. performances at the finish—Soames and Warburton.

Another subject recorded at some length by my ciné-camera was the preparation of our—that is, the M.G. Car Club Midland Centre's—1939 trial. We had lost the services of Alan Hunt, and the job of clerk-of-the-course was " wished " on to A. E. (Jim) Frost, recently co-opted on to our committee. We were also enjoying the services on the committee of Norman Grove, from the Hagley Club. To these two, jointly, must be given the credit for exploiting the Habberley Wood area, which lies south-west of Shrewsbury. From a metalled-surfaced approach lane, paths branched off in every direction through the woods. A number of the more likely looking were tried out, immense fun being obtained in the process.

In the film one sees, for example, Frank Kemp with the back wheels of his M.G. (one of the special 12 h.p.-engined series " T ") apparently in a ditch. All efforts to drive out or reverse out result only in the bodysides of the M.G. being plastered ever more thickly in glutinous mud. Again, one meets the Delingpole mackintosh, of which the rear seam is held by only a single thread top and bottom, the rest gaping wide open. Frost's Frazer-Nash-B.M.W. is seen " crabbing " to such an extent that it appears to climb a hill entirely sideways.

Bastock shows great prescience in giving an advanced preview of a sign since made world famous by Mr. Churchill, though exactly what victory Bastock had in mind in the halcyon days of 1938–39 I am not altogether sure.

The Motor Cycling Club played safe for the first plain-tyre " Exeter." A little too safe, I was told, but I was not on the trial myself in any capacity, neither as driver, passenger, nor spectator. Clifford Bridge, Higher Rill, Pin Hill (re-start), Harcombe (re-start), Woodhaynes, and Meerhay were the non-stop hills used in the first plain-tyre " Exeter." The ascent of Simms was made optional, success there cancelling out a failure on any one of the other hills, or qualifying the driver for a special Simms award if no other failures were recorded.

The " Exeter " brought to a close the highly successful career of the " Cream Cracker " M.G. team (Toulmin, Crawford, Jones). The team went out in a blaze of glory through their performance in this trial, taken together with the results of the other M.C.C. events through the season, giving them the 1938–39 Team Championship. This success was announced in the press on the very day that Toulmin got married—January 20th, 1939. An acceptable wedding gift !

Macdermid also announced a temporary withdrawal from active trials participation, and the fact, in addition, that he would be getting married in the early summer. His place in the " Musketeer " team was taken by Dickie Green.

To go back a bit, I had intended to take delivery of the new coupé on January 1st, 1939, but when advice reached me, a couple of weeks before Christmas, that the car was ready and waiting, I decided to get it into commission at once. A number of us from the Midland Centre of the M.G. Car Club were going

down to Hatfield on Saturday, December 17th, for a party being
" thrown " by the Main Centre, and I arranged with the M.G.
factory for the new car to be taken into Oxford and left at the
M.G. Garages for me to collect on my way home from Hatfield
on the Sunday. My wife and myself were going down to Hatfield
with my business partner Leonard Simmons, in his Triumph
Dolomite, and he was agreeable to making the necessary detour
through Oxford on the way home.

The party went off in tremendous style, not a " down-stage,"
but a light-hearted, free-and-easy affair. In the earlier part of
the evening George Monkhouse showed his super-all-colour films
of the 1938 Grand Prix Races. Later there was dancing and
general merriment, with a number of stunt competitions.

Arising out of one of these was an incident which, although
it has nothing to do with trials, featured a trials driver, and I
beg leave to relate it here, both as " light relief" from page
after page of wheelspin and special tests, and because the fine
sense of humour of the couple involved allows them always to
enjoy the re-telling of this anecdote.

One of the competitions was to find the lady with the most
dimpled knees, and to ensure strict impartiality the contestants
were ranged behind a screen, slung so that their faces and the
upper part of the body were covered, leaving the limbs on view.
A certain driver, recognizing, as he thought, his own wife's knees,
exhorted her to uncover them a little farther. You will at once
have guessed that the said driver picked on the wrong lady, and
you are right, *but* the wife to whom it was assumed the request
was being addressed was standing near. Recognizing her
husband's voice, and being a dutiful wife, she complied with the
request, although in her case the knees were fully revealed
already. The husband, seeing no response from the lady to
whom actually he was addressing his remarks, and being still
unaware of his error, called for further effort. As the wife was
already revealing a pair of fully-fashioned to their very tops,
she began to have considerable doubts, but bravely went a
shade farther. It was only when she was wondering fearfully
what further silken delights the competition was going to
necessitate her showing that realization dawned on both sides !

The following day was one of the coldest I remember, and
despite being five up in the Triumph, I never got warm. I was
the more dispirited, in consequence, when an intensive search

of the M.G. Garages at Oxford disclosed not a sign of the new coupé. There was, of course, no one at the factory on a Sunday, for me to try to find out where the error had crept in, so I sent off a post-card, after tea at the " Clarendon," and came home in the Triumph.

There was an apologetic trunk-call from Abingdon on Monday morning, and the coupé arrived in Birmingham that same afternoon.

I was not the only one making a change of car. In our own little circle Kenneth Delingpole disposed of the blown " PB " M.G. and purchased a 1½-litre H.R.G. Jim Frost changed the well-tried 1½-litre B.M.W. for one of the new T.T.-type 2-litre jobs, a machine also favoured by consistently successful L. G. Johnson, for the 1939 season.

The final stages of preparation for the M.G. Car Club Midland Centre's Trial were much enlivened by heavy falls of snow. There was snow lying thickly on the ground also when I went along as passenger, in Frank Kemp's 1½-litre-engined, series " T " M.G., to the Main Centre's Annual Chilterns Trial on January 29th.

The Midland Centre were flat out for the team award, and supporting Kemp were Norman Grove with his Arnott supercharged series " T," and Kenneth Rawlings, 1938 " Abingdon " winner, driving a standard series " T " belonging to his fiancée, Miss Edna Ison. The centre had a red-letter day. Kemp, whose trials luck had often been diabolical, had fortune smile on him for a change and, driving splendidly, won the race, and the Midland Centre team collected the award they had set out for.

At the start we talked with Philip and Lionel Flower. Philip was not amongst those who were making a change of car for the new year, continuing to put his faith in the old J2 which had brought him so far and so very successfully.

Dickie Green was there, too, and on this occasion was not competing, having taken on the job of marshal-in-charge at Rapid Rise. This was a comparatively new Chilterns " find," and one I had not seen, although I knew that it could be quite a " stopper." It stopped the entire entry that day, as, also, did the hill on private ground known as " Cookson's Stopper." In a previous trial this hill had been climbed by almost the entire entry, but on the present occasion the surface was virgin snow when the first man arrived.

Although the organizers were a little dispirited that months of work trying to seek a course which would baffle the clerk of the weather had proved of no avail, the destination of the main awards again having to be decided by the times in the driving tests, I enjoyed that trial a whole lot.

The same week-end the other members of the Midland Centre committee were a little concerned to find some of the hills for our trial blocked completely by snow, but this thawed out and dried away so effectively that, the night before the trial, we were praying for rain to put a " kick " into our course. Our prayers were answered at the eleventh hour. As we were trying to intimidate those competitors who were already assembled for the trial on the morrow, by showing them ciné-shots of members of the committee failing on various of the hills, someone rushed in to announce : " It's raining ! "

I had charge of the three sections in Habberley Wood, and while, undoubtedly, these hills provided plenty of good fun for competitors, there were not the failures we had hoped for, and which we should have had if the rain had started a little earlier and gone on a bit longer.

The rain did its stuff all right at Allez 'Oop. Only L. G. Johnson, with his new T.T. replica Frazer-Nash-B.M.W., climbed non-stop through all the sections into which we had divided this hill. After clearing up at Habberley, I arrived at Allez 'Oop just in time to see Alf Langley, wearing headgear exactly resembling an ordinary schoolboy's cap, literally fling the little " Grasshopper " Austin at the hill. Although he had two or three attempts, only one " official," of course, enjoying himself hugely, he could not emulate Johnson's splendid climb.

Ratlinghope, where we staged a re-start, saved us more awards than we had anticipated. I had a look at Horderley Hill. Just above the start the ruts had deepened, and although there were few actual failures here, some of the smaller cars went up at a remarkable angle, and fairly plastered themselves in mud.

These were the results we got out, not long after the finish :

Best Performance.—L. G. Johnson (1911 c.c. Frazer-Nash-B.M.W.).

Best under 1100 c.c.—W. H. Scriven (747 c.c. Austin s/c).

Best over 1100 c.c.—J. F. Guest (3622 c.c. Allard).

Kimber Team Trophy.—J. F. Guest, C. W. Taylor, K. A. Scales.

Inter-Centre Team Trophy.—North-Western Centre (Guest, Scales, J. F. Clent).

First-Class Awards.—J. A. Hallmark (M.G.) ; D. H. Jones (Ford) ; A. H. Langley (Austin) ; C. W. Taylor (M.G.) ; H. B. Woodhall (W.F. Special) ; D. Kane (M.G.) ; K. Scales (M.G.).

CHAPTER XIII

1939. *" Non-Stop "* *Ends*

THE coupé was now thoroughly run in, and I was itching to give it a run, and could not contain my patience until the " Land's End " came along. I saw what seemed the golden opportunity in the fact that the 1939 " Colmore " was divided into two parts—the Trophy Trial for sports cars and experienced drivers and the Goblet event for cars and drivers of a more modest calibre. The " Trophy," of course, was the type of event I was eliminating from my 1939 programme, but the Goblet seemed to be just the type of thing I had in mind when buying the coupé. In point of fact, however, I rather fell between two stools, because, whereas the car came under the heading of " a more modest calibre " all right, myself, the driver, came under the heading " experienced," which put me half-way into the Trophy event in theory, and I know that there were people who misconstrued my act in entering the Goblet section as plain " pot-hunting."

When the results showed that the coupé had been the only car to get round the Goblet course without loss of marks, I must admit that I was embarrassed, and I suggested to Alf Langley, the donor of the Goblet, that I should not take the award, but he insisted on my having it. The number of tankards of beer I had to buy that evening, to salve my conscience, was phenomenal.

" Dicing " with a " roof " on was an altogether new experience, not at all comparable to an open car with the hood raised, the feeling of being shut in being much greater.

Bownham, where I had watched so many good cars and drivers fail in the " Gloucester," was bad at first, but the mud seemed to come off and leave a firmer surface underneath after only a very few cars had tackled it, and thereafter gave little trouble, the coupé rocketing up in style, though to the detriment of the short running-boards, which form an extension of the swept front-wings on the series " T " M.G.

Where all the Goblet drivers, and quite a large number of the Trophy entrants also, went adrift was on the timed climb up

Stancombe. That the bogey time of 17 seconds for the climb was severe is shown by the fact that, out of the combined entry, there were nine drivers only who did not exceed the time allowance, and, of these, three needed the whole 17 seconds, and of the other six, only Allard beat 16 seconds. The coupé went up in 16·2 seconds, though when I look at the potentialities of many of the cars that were over the 17 seconds, I cannot for the life of me think how it was achieved.

Most difficult test of all for the Trophy cars was the re-start on Langley Hill, where Allard and Soames used 6·4 of the permitted 7 seconds and L. G. Johnson the whole 7 seconds, everyone else being outside the time limit.

So, for the second time in three years, Allard won the Colmore Trophy. This being the last pre-war " Colmore," let us have the results :

Colmore Trophy.—S. H. Allard (3622 c.c. Allard).
Best under 1100 c.c.—D. Murkett (939 c.c. M.G. s/c).
Best over 1100 c.c.—L. G. Johnson (1191 c.c. B.M.W.).
" Tailwaggers " Award.—K. C. H. Rawlings (847 c.c. M.G.).
Trial-to-Trial Trophy.—N. H. Grove (1292 c.c. M.G. s/c).
First-Class Award.—M. S. Soames (4379 c.c. Allard).
Second-Class Awards.—C. D. Buckley (Austin) ; P. S. Flower (M.G.) ; H. L. Hadley (Austin).
Seventeen Third-Class Awards.
Club Team Trophy.—Allard, Hutchison, Johnson.
One-Make Team Award.—Allard, Hutchison, Soames.

I realize that one could, to take an extreme case, write a book by merely stringing together a collection of " quotes " from the works of others, and I must confess I have been guilty of rather many " quotes " in this book. Many of them, however, have been from the excellent articles which used to be published every month in *The Sports Car* from the pen of R. A. Macdermid, and Mac had a way of summing up the trend of development in our sport in a manner on which I find it hard to improve. I take the liberty, therefore—and under war-time conditions I have not been able to contact Macdermid—of taking a slice out of his May 1939 article :

" With the competition-tyre days rapidly vanishing into the haze of memories and most of us settling down to trials under the new regime, it is possible now to assess the value of the restrictions which were to put our sport right with the world. The chief argument advanced in favour of the use of plain covers was that the old courses would no longer be possible, with a secondary pious hope that their use would attract novices to swell falling entry lists.

" And how is this panning out in practice ? Looking through the results of nearly every trial of importance this year, one is immediately struck by the recurrence of the phrases : ' No competitor succeeded in climbing this hill,' ' Only two managed to struggle through Section 1,' and ' Many were unable even to reach the starting-line.'

" Weather conditions are always blamed for the unexpected severity of the hills : heavy rain on the previous night, sometimes snow. Much more frequently than in the past, hills have to be abandoned as impossible, and we find almost a complete dearth of first-class awards, with an occasional awards list wherein the best performance attained only third-class standard.

" This state of affairs is understandable because much the same old courses are being used. It is indeed difficult to discover in what way the nuisance value is being lowered ; rather would it appear that organizers have been abandoned to the vagaries of the most fickle climate known to man. Rather late in the day it has been appreciated that to plot a weatherproof plain-tyre course is no mean task."

The Motor Cycling Club, wisely making no attempt to tone down their first plain-tyre " Land's End," used exactly the same route as for the 1938 event. This may seem in contradiction to Macdermid's remarks above, but the type of hill used by the M.C.C. for their long-distance classics is affected in only a very small degree by the weather.

Goodenough and I arranged to run in sequence again, and although we were not able to enjoy Green's company this time, since he was running with the " Musketeer " team, " the luck of the draw " threw into our company not only the very car in which Green had ridden with us in 1938, the blown " PB," MJ 9898 (now owned by Bud Murkett), but also Green's 1937 unblown series " T " Midget, BBM 1, now driven by Bill Taylor.

Quite a number of well-known drivers were seen behind strange steering-wheels in the 1939 " Land's End." Of the disbanded " Cream Cracker " team, Toulmin appeared with a 1935 four-seater " N " Magnette, Crawford with a 3½-litre S.S.

Jaguar " 100," both retaining clean sheets and securing Premier Awards. The " Grasshopper " Austins did not run, and Alf Langley competed on one of the new Austin Eights with full saloon bodywork. It is to his undying credit that he failed only at the re-start on the upper reaches of Bluehills, where the Austin just could not be got away. Scriven went through the trial in his everyday Austin Big Seven saloon, *but* with the " Grasshopper's " supercharger under the bonnet, and gained a Premier Award.

On the night section the coupé really came into its own, with its extra comfort and protection from the elements, although circumstances permitted of the night section on the 1939 " Land's End " being dealt with in an unusually satisfactory manner by Goodenough, Taylor, Murkett, and myself.

The night time-check was at the Paradise Garage and Roadhouse, about ten miles out of Bristol on the Bristol–Bridgwater road, and about a quarter of a mile past the Goodenough's home, so that we went straight through to there, and were then able to have a rest in the warmth and comfort of the Goodenough's lounge, the while Mr. and Mrs. regaled us with coffee, sandwiches, and cake. Thank you, Mrs. Goodenough.

It was obvious from the first crack of dawn that fine weather was going to be enjoyed, and there developed one of the finest and warmest Easters in many a long day.

I was glad to have the coupé top in the half-open position even before we got to the first hill, Station Hill, Lynton, although it was still quite early. Waiting here to make my attempt, I saw the ubiquitous V8 Ford engine in yet another new setting, under the bonnet of a T.T. Frazer-Nash.

It was no fault of the coupé's that a Premier Award was not secured. I made a really bosh shot at the Bluehills hairpin, pushing the front end up on to the sandbags hard enough to bend the axle beam slightly. It was the only blot on a grand " Land's End." Goodenough made quite sure about his time-checks this year and got his Premier.

Murkett also got his Premier, with the ex-Dickie Green " PB," but Taylor with the other ex-Green car failed the hairpin at Bluehills, not by fouling the outside of the corner as I had done, but stopping with spin through taking the corner too sharply, to avoid the sandbags.

The results also showed that Green was going to be an

adequate substitute for Macdermid in the " Musketeer " team, this trio taking the " Land's End " team award.

At the beginning of the year I had been elected to the committee of Sunbac, and from there co-opted on to the trials sub-committee. A decision had been taken not to hold the Team Trial, feeling that it could at best be a three-cornered contest, between the " Grasshopper " Austins, the " Musketeer " M.G.s, and the " Tailwagger " Allards. In its place we decided to have a " farthest-up " or " American " hill-climb, up the same ridge on which Red Daren lay, and combine with it a short trial for the " cars and drivers of a more modest calibre," much on the lines of the " Goblet " section of the " Colmore."

I was to have had the job of clerk of the course for this event, but it did not come off. While entries for the trial were meagre, they would have justified running it, but the hill-climb did not attract and it was decided not to run the one without the other.

Mit Harris struck out on entirely new lines for the "Abingdon," taking it right out of the Cotswolds and making a two-day run of it, also having a rally section.

On the first day the start was from the M.G. factory at Abingdon and competitors came up by main roads to Rushmere. Unfortunately, I had run the coupé into the back of a lorry, rather to its detriment, but managed to borrow an old Austin Seven to convey myself to Rushmere to watch the lads " dicing." A spell of fine weather had taken the sting out of Rushmere, and I was surprised that Harris had not set the starting-line nearer to the foot of the hill.

I exposed a good deal of ciné-film there during the afternoon, yet only one failure is recorded among my shots. I was delighted to see my old, ex-" Cracker," blown " PB," JB 7521 flash over the top. It had gone from me to the dealer through whom I had purchased the coupé, and had been immediately bought by another Birmingham driver, A. T. (Fred) Daniel. Daniel, however, had been having small fortune with the old car, and for the " Abingdon " had turned it over to Kenneth Rawlings, filling the rôle of passenger himself. Rawlings returned the " best performance under 1100 c.c."

I did not go on into Wales to see the rest of the trial next day, but I learned later that there was one real " stopper " used, called Swan Song, which was climbed by only three—Geoffrey

Mansell with the ex-Lloyd Jones V8-engined " Triangle," J. R. Lines (L.N. Special), also a Ford-engined machine, and Jack Terras on his blown " PB " Midget. Both Terras and Lines had lost marks elsewhere, so that only Mansell finished the trial with a clean sheet.

At Rushmere I saw that Toulmin's 1938 " Cream Cracker " car had passed into the hands of Ken Scales, well-known and very successful north-country driver, and, being always very interested in the careers of " cars with a history," discovered that Crawford's car of the same team also had a new owner, in the person of C. M. Davis. The third car was still in J. E. S. Jones's hands.

If it had not been for my unfortunate contretemps with the lorry, which rendered the coupé *hors de combat* for above three weeks, I think that I should have gone on the " Lawrence." It had always been one of my favourite trials, and although the W.D. hills are very steep and loose, and no doubt the coupé would have come gently to a stop on a number of them, the surfaces were not damaging. However, a decision whether or not to go was made for me, and, lacking suitable alternative transport, I was not able even to fill the rôle of spectator.

Norman Terry competed with the " Terryford," and he told me that the " Lawrence " was as good as ever. On the assumption—a correct one, as it turned out—that the use of plain tyres would make less difference on the W.D. hills than on most types of trials hill, virtually the same course as in the previous year was used. In fact the " Lawrence " seems to have been one of the better trials of 1939, and hugely enjoyed by those who took part, so much so that Terry told me that several hills were tackled again, after the trial proper had finished officially.

Honours fell to M. H. Lawson, on the white H.R.G., who beat Terry by a short head.

It seems that by not going on the 32nd " Edinburgh," at Whitsun, I missed one of the best of the series, but I had fixed my summer holiday rather early, wanting to take a particular cruise itinerary which was not being repeated at all later in the year. In consequence I was sailing from Tilbury, on the *Stratheden*, headed for Venice, much about the time competitors were setting out on the " Edinburgh."

The trial was favoured with brilliant weather, although this did not, judging by the results list, entirely take the sting out of

Adderstonshiels. This hill and the other one in the Scottish section, Costerton, are a couple of observed sections which, to my regret, I have not seen, but I was led to understand that Adderstonshiels, in particular, was quite good fun. Dickie Green, Jack Bastock, and Arch Langley followed up their " Land's End " success by winning the team award again, and it seems likely that if the season had run its course, these three drivers would have taken the 1939 Team Championship.

My early holiday also caused me to miss the Blackpool Rally. This event had lapsed in 1938, owing to the fact that the R.A.C. had chosen Blackpool as the terminal point for their national rally in that year, and the Lancashire Automobile Club had not thought it wise to have a second event of similar type there in the same season. The 1939 event was run on almost the identical plan that had proved so popular in 1937, though there was one novel feature in an award for the best combined performance in both the rally itself and in the coachwork competition which followed. This award was taken by D. B. Hall with a very smart drop-head coupé body on a Ford V8 chassis. Best performer in the rally itself was W. C. N. Norton, with a 3½-litre S.S. Jaguar " 100," a car for which, I must confess, I have always had a very soft spot in my heart.

Chief " gaffer " of the Blackpool Rally was Maurice Toulmin. The hard work put in by him in reviving this event, after its year's lapse, was rewarded with an entry of 150. It was the more unfortunate, therefore, that after the road section on the Friday had been run off in very fine weather, there should have been a steady drizzle all the time the final tests were being undertaken at Blackpool on the Saturday morning.

On Saturday, June 17th, I drove in my last competitive event, not a trial, but the Singer Club's driving tests, again held in Victoria Park, Leamington Spa.

Compared with the very enjoyable afternoon spent there in 1938, the whole thing seemed a bit thin. Probably it was the threatening weather that prompted the organizers to have the three tests in operation simultaneously. The fact, also, that the third test, the " awkward garage " one, in which I had come adrift in 1938, was replaced by a shorter, simpler affair of running to the car, starting up, accelerating to, and braking astride, a line, and that, furthermore, there was a much reduced entry, made the whole event appear to be over almost before it had started. It was one of the shortest, most quickly finished events I remember. Proceedings were enlivened, however, by Norman Terry, who competed in an S.S. Jaguar " 100," and cheerfully cast pylons and barriers all over the park.

Under the eagle eye of Alf Langley and his wife I slid the coupé in and out of the " garages " in the first test to make fastest time (closed-car class), but at the second test wished heartily that I had dropped the coupé top and run in the open-car class. The blind rear-quarters, always the weakness of this type of body, made it physically impossible to sight the second " garage " until the car was almost on top of it, it then being found, of course, that the car was in entirely the wrong position to be coaxed into the wretched " garage."

I managed to display sufficient agility in the third test to record fastest closed-car time again, and this and my success in the first test offset the very poor time recorded on the second test to a sufficient degree to give me best performance in the closed-car class.

My old friend W. C. (Bill) Butler was best Singer Club performer, Dennis Flather, with a B.M.W. instead of the " vintage " Brescia Bugatti, best visitor. Best under 1100 c.c. was A. C. Westwood (Ballila Fiat), whom I did not remember having seen engaged actively in competition for quite a time, and best over 1100 c.c., Kenneth Rawlings on Miss Ison's series " T " M.G.

The much-reduced entry was not all due to the general conditions and calls of national service. A number of drivers had gone down to Bristol for Macdermid's wedding, and several of these went on that night to Bridgwater, to run next day in the " Brighton–Beer."

The " Beer," which used to draw entries of more than a hundred, could only muster thirty. The event might well have started and finished at Widlake, since the other hills, Windout, Fingle, and Simms, gave no trouble, but Widlake was climbed only by Hutchison. There was an excellent attempt by L. G. Johnson with the T.T. replica B.M.W. : he actually got the front wheels past the " Observed Section Ends," but as the hill was not graded at all, this gave him no advantage over those who failed low down. So long as one man climbs a hill, I suppose the inclusion of that section is justified, but one still felt that Widlake, like Juniper, was not a hill for plain-tyre trials, except when bone-dry, and in our fickle climate, who could say when that would be ?

About the last of the one-time classics to be run before the war-clouds broke was our old, light-hearted friend, the " Barnstaple."

The " Barnstaple " touched bottom ; the entries fell to sixteen, while up to the eleventh hour no observers and officials were available at all ! However, the trial did take place ; it did, as was almost traditional, get mixed up with the local hunt, so that one test could not be staged, and it added yet another to the long list of successes piled up by my very good friend and " best man," Dickie Green.

Well, those were the trials years, as I said in the preface, the happiest of my life. That there was much that was not well with our little world at the time at which the sport was brought to a summary conclusion I have not tried to conceal.

One can but hold an open mind about the first (nearly) full season of plain-tyre trials. Too many outside influences were at work for a full inquest. That world conditions, with the calls of national service, were in large measure responsible for the small entry lists in many events was unquestionable. I was a little surprised, and rather disappointed, when the Motor Cycling Club decided not to hold the Torquay Rally in 1939 : it was the rally-type events that were getting the entries.

No man can say when, or in what conditions, it will be possible to set our sport going again, but it is reasonable to suppose that the M.C.C. long-distance classics will be among the very first events to be revived, and when the " Land's End " is run again, I shall be there, even if I have to take the Rover Twelve saloon which is my war-time " mount " (the coupé being disposed of). You don't have to have a " Special " to get to Land's End, and if you stop on a hill or two, which the Rover most definitely would, there is little likelihood of " bending " the motor, so here's hoping.

INDEX